LEADERSHIP LESSONS

FROM A LIFE OF CHARACTER AND PURPOSE IN PUBLIC AFFAIRS

Stephen S. Kaagan

University Press of America, Inc.
Lanham • New York • London

Copyright © 1997 by
University Press of America,® Inc.
4720 Boston Way
Lanham, Maryland 20706

3 Henrietta Street
London, WC2E 8LU England

ISBN 0-7618-0642-3 (cloth: alk: ppr.)

To my four children,

Jenny, Steven, Kyle and David.

It is their future that concerned me as I wrote this book.

Contents

Foreword

The characters of the individuals involved in public matters do affect the course of history. Gregory Anrig was deeply involved in public matters and his character influenced the outcome of those matters. His official responsibilities included being a school Principal, a school system Superintendent, Commissioner of Education of Massachusetts, and head of Educational Testing Service. Those public matters he influenced included the quest for quality of treatment in education, regardless of race or gender; the encouragement and measurement of educational achievement; the integration of non-English speaking and special needs students into regular public education; the balancing of the tension between national authority and local autonomy; and addressing the special problems of urban education, from school financing to the disintegration of family structures. Like most issues of great weight, these matters were worked through in a series of small, routine decisions, as well as more momentous ones, under Gregory Anrig's leadership. These matters are of significance to what sort of people and nation we are and will be. Gregory Anrig understood that significance.

It is appropriate, then, to ask about the character of Gregory Anrig. He was a very good man, a man loved and respected. Fairness and giving all concerned a chance to be be heard were concepts which came from so deeply within him as to marrow-born. He was fun and funny, with a ready chuckle and an appreciative smile. He was optimistic and believed in the likelihood of good outcomes, especially if you worked at it. Unconcerned with his own importance, he recognized and demonstrated respect for all with whom he dealt. All were treated with dignity. He was not self-indulgent; his own emotions rarely played a role in his decision making. He was honest and more. "Integrity" is a word often used to describe him. He faced hard issues and did not attempt to shift them to others. He believed and acted on the belief that the obligations of one's life were far greater than mere self interest. Gregory Anrig kept in his office the journal of Horace Mann, the great educator. He believed profoundly in what Mann said: "Be ashamed to die until you have won some victory for humanity." Gregory Anrig did win victories for humanity.

There are other good, warm, funny, well-liked men of integrity. Why is Gregory Anrig nonetheless special? Two strong answers emerge from the many which spring forward.

The first is that Gregory Anrig was remarkably effective. He was a leader and very successful at it. His ability to work with others was almost uncanny. He drew from others their best qualities, without ever catering to falsity in his relationships, through flattery or overstatement. He was firmly in charge and still provided others with access and real participation. He made others believe they had the capacity to meet his expectations. Those expectations were high and were clearly articulated. Like other great leaders, Gregory Anrig valued the role of civility in maintaining discourse. George Washington attempted to live by certain rules, the first of which was this: "Every action done in company ought to be done with some sign of respect to those that are present." Gregory Anrig practiced that rule daily.

Enormously difficult issues came to him for decision. He did not avoid them and how he handled them provides a model. When, during the Boston school desegregation crises other elected officials attempted to avoid their responsibilities, Gregory Anrig met his. Gregory Anrig taught, by example, such lessons to all of us who worked with him. The lessons of his leadership are worthy of analysis and description.

Secondly, Gregory Anrig showed that government can be a force for good and, the corollary, that good men need not be corrupted by the power of public office. Civic virtue and personal virtue not only coexisted in Gregory Anrig, they strengthened each other. The story of Gregory Anrig's life is an antidote to cynicism about government. Some historians credit the artistic Renaissance as starting with a mural, dating to the 1300's, in the Palazzo Pubblico, the seat of government in Sienna. The fresco by Ambrogio Lorenzetti celebrates the Republic and depicts "The Virtues of Good Government" in contrast with "The City-State Under Tyranny." The good government brings peace, justice, and prosperity to the people. The bad government brings desolation, injustice, war and famine. Gregory Anrig believed in government as a force for the good. Earl Long, the flamboyant Louisiana politician, populist and demagogue, once was asked whether he believed in good government. After a pause, he answered "Pretty good." While appreciating Earl Long's humor, Gregory Anrig would find that his answer was simply not good enough. Gregory Anrig thought the people deserved the best in their government. He tried and did give his best.

Sandra L. Lynch
U.S. Circuit Court Judge
U.S. Court of Appeals for the First Circuit
September, 1996

Acknowledgments

I want to acknowledge the assistance of several individuals and organizations. First is the incalculable support supplied by the Anrig family. Unyielding confidence in me and the ready availability of personal papers are but two of the forms this assistance took. The Educational Testing Service was very helpful, providing access to key people and offsetting the costs of necessary travel. A Spencer Foundation Grant was critical as research and rewriting progressed. Two Michigan State University colleagues deserve special mention, Dr. Diane Holt-Reynolds, who helped me locate my voice in the telling of the story and made innumerable editorial suggestions, and Cathy Siebert, who did copy editing, proofreading and formatting. I also owe a great debt to the individuals who consented to be interviewed. Eleanor Horne of ETS and Mike Daly of Massachusetts were especially helpful here. Finally, I want to thank my mate, Susan Sundquist. While it is difficult to get a project underway, it is much more difficult to complete it. The oasis we have found made closing a lot easier.

Chapter 1

BRINGING LIFE TO ISSUES

> *"We must understand how the past affects us, we should keep the present full of rich and satisfying experiences, and we should devote some energy each day to building for the future. Just as a river can be said to have parts that cannot be clearly divided, so too should we consider the whole of our time when deciding how to spend our lives."*
>
> *Deng Ming-Dao 1992, #15*

Public affairs unfold over time through a dynamic and intricate interweaving of issues and persons, issues that command public attention and persons who take on and are swept up in these issues. This book is an account of two journeys, each involving an intersection of persons and issues. First is the journey of Gregory R. Anrig, a public affairs leader who died in 1993 after thirty years of service to American Education. As the following pages will attest, his leadership in public affairs embraced a set of consequential and enduring issues. Second is my own journey through Anrig's life. The meaning I garnered from his life reflects deeply on my own and on the issues that will dominate my future work.

The message of this book is that competent and principled public affairs leadership is possible: that organizations meant to do so can indeed keep the public trust and serve the best interests of their constituents. The book's medium is the working life of one prominent twentieth century leader and educator, Gregory R. Anrig - what he said and did, how others interpreted his words and actions, and the yield from my own experiences and conversations with him.

That the readers of this book may not recognize Anrig's name, know who he was or what he did, is not consequential. His lack of public prominence is frankly an asset for my purposes. I fully intend to plumb it as a compelling reason that readers should come to believe that they can emulate in their work and worlds what he did in his.

Too much of the literature on leadership is about people whose working lives seem remote and inaccessible to their fellow citizens on whom we depend for the effective functioning of our society.   These thousands of individuals who manage governmental organizations at the federal, state and local levels need a clearer vision of what quality leadership entails. So too do the thousands who hold key positions in non-governmental or non-profit organizations. While not part of the government structure per se, many of them carry out as much of a public agenda as any government agency. So I offer here lessons from the life of a person in whose work shoes others can walk.

The book is organized into nine chapters. Each includes stories and themes of Anrig's life arranged largely in chronological order. Some stories and themes could almost stand alone; others integrate easily with a larger whole. None necessarily makes a center around which the others fit, but their sum propounds a larger significance that offering them up chronologically may obscure. That larger significance lies in a rich array of telling lessons for us in the broad reaches of public affairs leadership.

Though I know little about sewing (and do less), writing about Anrig's life, of threading together public moments, private tales and character-revealing scenes, has seemed remarkably like "writing a quilt." As you the reader examine the pieces of the quilt, you will see that each has its own color, texture, size and shape. In stitching the pieces together, I intended that they comprise one large square of cloth that would offer a single coherent perspective.

As I proceeded with the writing I sought in particular to show how the quilt pieces were set against the well-defined background of a small number of consequential social issues that dominated Anrig's attention over the three decades of his work life. Four issues stand out. They include:

- the paramount role of teaching and learning in schooling;
- equality of educational opportunity;
- the balance among local, state and federal authority for schooling; and
- assessment of educational progress, especially the assessment of student performance.

These four issues occupied his considerable energies and attention from the mid-sixties to the mid-nineties. Interestingly they were to one extent or another very much at the front of the public's mind during that time. The first, the paramount role of teaching and learning, might strike the reader as almost an "elaboration on the obvious." A normal reaction would be that all people who work in and around schools concur that teaching and learning is what education is all about.

The lamentable truth is that while most people might agree rhetorically, their actions would likely speak another truth. For many, schooling is really about getting young people out of their parents' hair, or keeping them off the streets, or delaying their entry into the job market, or even offering sports opportunities to a few gifted youngsters.

Like welfare, healthcare and other important social functions, education is an endeavor in which all connected with it struggle to remind themselves of what is basic and central to it. Anrig was one who repeatedly insisted that the essential and primary function of schools was teaching the young a variety of skills and capacities they needed to function as adults.

The second, equality of educational opportunity, has endured as one of the most volatile and visible issues in the public arena. It has not only affected many lives, it has in the recent past claimed several. In the late fifties and early sixties the issue riveted the attention of the whole country for protracted periods. The events at Little Rock's Central High School in 1957 and at the University of Alabama in 1963 are a sufficient reminder.

Gary Orfield, noted national expert on school integration, observed that the quest of Black citizens in the late sixties for their civil rights changed the South permanently in fundamental ways. After the heyday of the Civil Rights Movement, the region was transformed both socially and economically. Central to this transformation was the admission of Black students to previously all white schools and universities (Orfield 1994).

The third, the balance of authority among governmental levels, might be a less visible issue, but it is no less volatile. For the last three decades there has been an unending cacophony of voices lamenting the loss of local decision making authority over schools. Swirling around in this persistent witch's pot have been a host of ingredients, from school district consolidation to the appropriate education of disabled students to the teaching of creationism. The basic issue is which level of government is in charge of what. What should local school boards be able to decide without intervention from the state or the federal government? Over what areas should the state have province? What say, if any, might the federal government have?

The fourth issue, assessment of educational progress and student performance, touches a sensitive chord in all of us. For most students it is a cause of anxiety, for some parents a cause of anger, for almost all school officials a source of constant aggravation. Who measures up to what set of standards; who sets the standards and how is performance measured? Do the measurement tools in fact measure what they are supposed to? Even if they do, are they fair to all groups or do they discriminate against some? Questions like these have dominated public discussion about assessment in the last three decades, and they are likely to remain front and center in the years ahead.

Over the thirty year period examined here, these four issues attained first line status as policy considerations on the national scene. But they did so at different times. Interestingly, there is a near even fit between the timing of the prominence in the public consciousness of three of the four issues and their prominence in the major segments of Anrig's professional career. Each one of the three had a lead role on the national stage, almost one after the other, in ten year periods from the mid-sixties to the mid-nineties. Similarly, each had a large role in Anrig's work as he moved through positions of increasing responsibility over the same period.

While these three issues did indeed become salient in both the public's eyes and Gregory Anrig's career one after the other as the 60's, 70's and 80's unfolded, their actual lines of development were considerably more organic, more holistic. All three, for example, were in fact active elements in the last two assignments Anrig had. For purposes of clarity, however, I present the issues as if they emerged chronologically, one after the other in bold relief.

In the first ten years of his career Anrig attained a firm grounding in education at the local level, as a teacher, school principal and district superintendent. These years convinced him that the heart of schooling was teaching and learning. They also helped him solidify an airtight commitment to equality of educational opportunity. He took these two commitments to Washington, D.C. in the Great Society years and landed an assignment where he was able to act on them.

In the succeeding ten years, imbued with these two fundamental commitments, he acted on a set of ideas about proper local, state and federal roles for schooling. He believed that the shaping of a fit balance among governmental levels was necessary to fulfill the requisite of equality of opportunity and affirm the centrality of teaching and learning. His chosen niche on the matter of shared governance was an assignment at the state level, wedged as it was between "federal concern" and "local control." Massachusetts in the 70's was the venue he selected.

In the last ten years of his career he brought what he had learned about the importance of teaching and learning, equality of opportunity and shared governance into his stewardship of educational assessment. His part - which came at a critical juncture - was to straighten out and begin to reshape the world's foremost educational assessment organization, the Educational Testing Service (ETS).

That there was coincidence between the prominence of these issues in the public's mind and in the major phases of Anrig's career is, in fact, no coincidence at all. Whereas it was indeed true for Anrig - and for all of us - that opportunities serendipitously present themselves, he consciously chose to work on these three issues. He did this while staying firmly attached to the preeminence of teaching and learning. His selection of which issues to work on and when, which commitments to keep and for how long, encapsulates a brand of leadership, the dynamics of which are important to understand. A major intent of this book is to reveal some of these dynamics.

Leadership also entails working on issues that in and of themselves offer up possibilities for leadership work. Each of the major issues Anrig chose to concern himself with, in its own way, has inherent leadership mettle. Each has its own set of tensions which when played out in the public arena result in social change. Teaching, for example, is in many senses equivalent to leadership; both involve coaching and coaxing fellow humans out of a state of not knowing. The word "educate "after all comes from Latin and means "to lead out from." When teaching works it beckons people to become more mentally active, to make connections and thereby take more informed action than they might have otherwise. These are the very same things enlightened leaders do with people they are attempting to lead.

Inherent in the issue of equality of educational opportunity is the quest for a state of affairs that does not presently exist. The issue concerns fair treatment for all, a condition that has never been present, but has been and will continue to be fervently sought for a long time. To seek equality of opportunity for fellow citizens is to assume leadership, because it is empowering for them and adds to their leverage to contribute to society.

The balance of local, state and federal authority for schooling is exactly that, a balance - and a very delicate one indeed. More than any other, this matter of shared responsibility for societal functions like education is a deep mystery to non-Americans.   They see our approach to governance as engendering chaos. In our more pessimistic moments, some of us may agree. In more optimistic ones, the blending of local, state and federal roles appears dynamic and capable of producing uniquely productive solutions to very difficult social problems. Struggling with this balance is integral to taking leadership. Determining the balance results in assigning responsibilities for important tasks and then cooperatively carrying them out.

Assessment as an activity exists because we want to know how well or poorly people are accomplishing important functions and programs are fulfilling essential tasks. The questions assessment poses are asked because we know we need to do better, to change, to improve. The function of assessing equates with the assumption of leadership because its results can lead us to new and more effective directions and strategies - with individuals, programs and policies.

As much as other human beings were Anrig's companions, associates and colleagues throughout his life, so too were these three issues. He lived and worked intimately with, beside and among them. They inscribe his most marked contributions to education and more broadly underline much of what he added to our store of knowledge about public affairs leadership.

The issues are as much pieces of our contemporary fabric as they were of Anrig's professional life. While their texture, contour and dimension inevitably changed over the duration of his career and even since his death a few years ago, they remain vibrant and dynamic concerns in our lives today. We are presently faced with choices about how they fit with the quilts we are stitching now. The same is likely to be true tomorrow. So I invite you as reader to take notice in the pages that follow of the weave of these issues in the total fabric that made up Anrig's life. At the same time I ask you to join with me in doing the important work of tracing their impact on our own lives and speculating on how our future work on them might reflect the quality of leadership we choose to court in the years ahead.

At a time in our history when so many in our nation decry the low quality of public affairs leadership, Anrig's life speaks eloquently to a set of requisites that cry out for fulfillment if our democracy is to survive. The manner in which he cradled and nurtured the public trust; the authentic relationships he had with other human beings; his ability to walk in other people's shoes - from these we can carry away lessons for improving the dynamics of public interactions that affect the welfare of all citizens. Learning them and applying them appropriately, we can change our destiny.

As noted earlier, Anrig's deeds rarely made the front page. His name was not a household word. It is this secondary positioning on the public stage that makes his life a useful instrument for our learning. His image was life size and real, and his legacy therefore more at the level of the graspable, the available, the attainable. We can take from his life more lessons with direct applicability than one might from the life of a person regarded as larger than life itself. And a story that offers more familiar content and context has the potential for engendering more hope in us as we struggle with the complex social issues that confront us.

As I arranged the quilt squares of this tale I first lay in some of the smaller squares of cloth. In a chapter entitled "Leadership Character" I reflect on his attributes as a public person and how they translate into leadership mettle. In particular there are perspectives on what it was like to be in his presence, in a physical, mental, and even moral and spiritual sense. These patches include others' testimony and vignettes that exemplify important values and concepts. In a companion chapter entitled "Leadership Headwaters", I describe his early years, the origins of his commitments, beliefs and professional modus operandi.

Then I insert larger squares. These are intended to illuminate the way the major education issues of his time framed and defined his brand of public affairs leadership. The chapter entitled "Attending to Civil Rights" traces the development of his thinking and recounts his performance on behalf of equality of educational opportunity. This segment covers the entirety of his professional career, not just the first ten years.

The chapter, "Massachusetts Service", highlights the particular part he played in the emergence of the state's roles in influencing the quality of schooling. While it covers only an eight year period, it traces the wide array of leadership capacities Anrig demonstrated in a position of responsibility and challenge.

"Reestablishing the Educational Testing Service", the last of the larger squares, focuses on how he revitalized an essential and unique educational organization, one in considerable distress at the time he took leadership of it. This chapter, like the one that precedes it, depicts the range and diversity of his leadership capabilities.

Toward the end of the text in a chapter entitled "Currents of Leadership", I examine how Anrig's approach to public affairs leadership fits into the way present day thinkers view the challenges of societal and organizational leadership. Then I review the major lessons of his life for public affairs leadership. There are two sections that do this. The first is called "Lessons From Living Public Affairs Leadership." It focuses on the lessons we can learn from the way he conducted himself as a public affairs leader. The second, entitled "Leadership Lessons From Working the Issues," ponders the instructive aspects of his role as shaper of policy in education.

In "Closings" I first summarize Anrig's major contributions and then encapsulate what I believe to be the essential meaning of his life. These concluding thoughts are drawn from a talk I gave in which I attempted to find a theme that infused all that he did and was, from his work on social issues to his familial relationships.

Finally, almost as an appendix, I add in some miniature squares, called "Anrigisms." Although tiny bits of cloth, they may represent the "hidden treasure" of this patchwork. These are the turns of phrase he borrowed from mentors - wholecloth or in part - or coined himself, to convey his perspective on important issues. They comprise only a few pages, but capture the unique way he used words and phrases to impress his ideas on those with whom he worked. They are telling emblems of values and characteristics discussed much more fully elsewhere in the text. Perhaps when he first proffered them, he thought them useful for a few exchanges at best. Instead they became permanent fixtures, good for repeated lightness in the midst of tense and difficult situations. At the very least they are intended to create the same effect on the quilt taken as a whole.

Many of the pieces of the quilt are my own stories. Some came to me as story squares already woven by another whose identity I can pass along as the source of the material. Other contributors wished to remain anonymous.

Chapter 2

Leadership Character

"Public servants are more readily the subject of charges, but if you know yourself you have done what you should, then such charges can't hit home. If charges alone make honest people shy away from public service, then those that will be left in government will be those likely to be deserving of charges. Having others believe in your integrity is damn important, but even more important is believing in it yourself and being willing to take on any irresponsible charge that comes along without being distracted." This excerpt is taken from a four-page handwritten letter Anrig wrote to me in 1978 after I had endured a day-long police interrogation. At the end of the experience I had telephoned him and said that I never wanted anything more to do with public service after what I had just been through. The interchange between us came on the heels of a criminal indictment of a top official of the Massachusetts Department of Education who had absconded with public funds. When nabbed, the official turned state's evidence on fifteen of his alleged accomplices. As a parting gesture, he then attempted to implicate me.

It is 1976 and the Massachusetts Department of Education is in the grips of ominous circumstance. A handful of staff have begun to surmise that a high ranking official of the Department is abusing his office after only eighteen months on the job. The likelihood is that he has stolen a large amount of money from the public purse. At first the staff thought that this official was merely exhibiting bad judgment; now there are signs emerging that he is engaged in something more like malfeasance.

Such scenes would not have been unusual in the mid-seventies for a host of other Massachusetts agencies. Government graft had been a fixture of the state political and bureaucratic scene for years. But Anrig, who heads the Department, and his colleagues, have been making a concerted attempt to clean up the Agency and keep it clean. No patronage posts in this Department for the relatives of state legislators. No insistence that employees of the Department buy high-priced tickets to testimonial dinners honoring elected officials. No sweetheart deals on state contracts for relatives of legislators or executive agency appointees.

Now this. Anrig has been Commissioner for over three years. They have been three tough years, with desegregation of the Boston Schools and a number of perplexing issues. This late afternoon gathering is intended as a moment of critical decision making on a matter that might be as complex and demanding as enforcing the due process clause of the U.S. Constitution against a wall of local community resistance.

Two chief deputies, of which I was one, the Department's General Counsel and the Chair of the Board to which Anrig reported, attend the meeting. The topic is the extent of the filth that has infiltrated the Department and how to go about cleaning it up. We sit in arm chairs and sofa ringing a coffee table. Anrig is the obvious focus of attention for the other four. He alternates between hunching forward in his chair with his elbows gently on its arms and extending backward, placing his feet on the top of the coffee table legs straight out. He puffs at a cigar, calm but intent. His head is straight, cheeks full and chin set but relaxed.

The first item for discussion is two contracts that are up for final sign off. I lead off with the assertion that the people listed to do the work in the contract are not qualified to do so. Anrig knows the people involved and recognizes that what I am saying is true. Yet he indicates with the tilt of his head that he is dubious, not necessarily disbelieving, just skeptical. Perhaps it is difficult for him to digest the full implication.

The flow of the meeting proceeds until Mike Daly, also a Deputy, punctuates the air with the contention that the situation could be very problematic. He says to Anrig, in essence, that this horse may well ride over you if you fail to ride it. The metaphor, crude as it is, seems to rivet Anrig's attention. He pulls his torso up more nearly straight in the chair, his elbows now embedded in the arms. Cigar puffs come at a slightly more rapid clip than before.

Finally, after some mutual meandering around possibilities and implications, Board Chair Chuck Grigsby inserts a suggestion for action: commission an investigative audit of the contracts and see what it turns up. Up to now Anrig's facial expression has changed little, even though there are evident signs of increasing tension, even pain. For over a half hour he has said almost nothing, asking only one or two brief questions. But the elbows are now nearly buried in the cushiony arms. There is no more alternating between sitting up straight and lounging forward. The jaw seesaws horizontally across tightly leveraged joints. And the skin tones of the back of the neck have shifted from characteristic red to uncharacteristic white.

On the heels of the last suggestion, the intensity recedes slightly and Anrig begins to show some signs of acquiescence. The slow hydraulic of chin and jaw eases. But clearly he still resists with full bodied emotion and spirit the obvious subtext of the conversation. How could a person whose job involved the support of students in school possibly breach the public trust like that? It is for him a nearly inconceivable outcome, extraordinarily difficult to accept.

Looking in on these proceedings, a casual observer might conclude that there were multiple routes out of the tight circumstances described above:

- keep our eyes open and wait to see what happens next; or
- take quick and harsh administrative action immediately such as firing the official, thereby nipping this in the bud; or

• • • • get more information so as to get to the bottom
of this, and then take definitive action to excise
it from the organization.

For Anrig, however, there was only one way to release
the tight hold that the public trust had on the frame of his mind:
direct and definitive application of due process.   Little else
beside this pillar of American political culture could have
displaced that other imperative, the inviolability of the public trust.

In the wake of this meeting Anrig engaged without delay
investigative auditors to look into the two suspicious contracts.
After hundreds of hours over several months, the auditors had
tracked every transfer of funds within the confines of two small
contracts, roughly fifty thousand dollars each. They followed the
trail of every invoice drawn and every check issued, from original
source to ultimate receiver. The total cost of the financial probes
nearly exceeded the cost of one of the targeted contracts. At
the end of their work it appeared very likely that the head of
occupational education and several others close to him had
abused their offices, by stealing over a million dollars.   Public
money had gone through strange hands and wound up in even
stranger places, including bank accounts in the names of
deceased people.

As soon as the facts started to come to light, Anrig asked
officers of the Governor's White Collar Crime Unit to pursue a full
criminal investigation of the matter. Immediately he went in front
of press and media representatives and disclosed all the
information he could within the constraints imposed by the
pending inquiry. According to Muriel Cohen, the <u>Boston Globe</u>
reporter who covered the story, she had never seen Anrig so
forthcoming with information as he was during this episode. Nor,
she said, had he appeared so troubled by a set of events as
these were shaping up to be (Cohen 1994).

The criminal investigation that ensued eventually yielded
a prison term for the principal perpetrator and assorted
indictments and convictions for others associated with him in the
illicit acts. For Anrig and his staff it resulted in several years of
distraction from other key tasks.   The State Department of

Education was already a beleaguered agency. Now it had suffered another "bloody nose."

Quickly Anrig and his top staff imposed procedures within the Department intended to prevent recurrences of such abuse. Some of the procedures made sense and were helpful. Others were Draconian, their prophylactic effect much less than their temporary public relations value. For me there was a harrowing day of interrogation by State Police investigators, topped off by a "voluntary" polygraph exam, and a "chance" meeting with the prosecutor to see if I was willing to testify before the Grand Jury. After all this, the trumped up allegations were dropped and I returned to the relative quietude of my new assignment as a university administrator in Brooklyn, New York.

The way the scandal was handled yielded no net loss in the credibility of the Commissioner within other sectors of state government or among the constituents of the Agency. Remarkably the media response, while direct, was not disabling. Those who violated the public trust were caught, afforded due process and punished. Some of the stolen funds, totalling over a million and half dollars were retrieved, most were not.

More than anything else, the actions described above are testimony to the power of honesty and forthrightness in public affairs. The specific setting in which they took place was that of a public agency out on a limb on a set of controversial issues. The general context was an environment polluted by chronic venality of public officials in high positions and the inveterate skepticism of a seasoned corps of media representatives.

The results could have been very different indeed. The crooks might not have been caught; positions the Department was taking on tough issues, however worthy, could have been compromised. Anrig and several other decent and competent people could have lost their jobs. The trust of many citizens in government agencies and officials, already low, could have reached even lower levels. In sum, things could have turned out a lot worse than they did. This very idea, of keeping the bad from turning into the worse, may point to one of the most profound responsibilities of the effective public servant - to keep a looming disaster from turning into an irretrievable catastrophe. Perhaps a course in how to do this should be built into every graduate program in public administration. Alternatively, one could keep reading, immersing oneself in the being, the doings and the sayings of the principal character presented here.

Who in fact was he? To start with, what kinds of professional background had he had before he came to be tested by situations like the one just described? What did his resume include under the heading, Professional Experience? Right before becoming Commissioner of Education for the Commonwealth of Massachusetts in 1973, he had spent three years at the University of Massachusetts at Boston. There he had led an effort to establish an Institute for Teaching and Learning. This offshoot of a young urban campus was intended as a new form of a "school of education". It had no set faculty, but rather flexible faculty resources deployed to assist with urban school problems.

This short stint in Boston had been a useful transition from a fast-paced four years in Washington, D.C. There, in the late sixties he had established within the U.S. Office of Education (now Department of Education), a unit to provide technical assistance to local school districts on civil rights compliance. In his last year or so in Washington he also served as chief aide to a noble but ill-fated Nixon appointee, Dr. James Allen. The White House fired Allen as Commissioner of Education for his outspoken opposition to U.S. military action in Cambodia during the Vietnam War. Even before that, Allen's liberal position on such matters as school desegregation had made him less than a favorite of the increasingly conservative architects of social policy in the White House.

Prior to his Washington service Anrig had been the superintendent of a rural school district, Williamstown in Western Massachusetts, from 1964 to 1967; and a school principal from 1960 to 1964 in an urban district, White Plains, New York. In the same district, but at a different school, he had served as a history teacher and principal's assistant from 1956 to 1960.

As is true with most people, a cursory rendering of Anrig's professional experiences tells only a fraction of the story. His physical characteristics, mental capacities, and moral and spiritual attributes commanded considerable attention and warrant ample description. He was on very first impression a physically imposing man. Wide shouldered and portly, and not particularly tall, he was clearly not an aspiring marathon runner. Nonetheless his generous girth was surprisingly well distributed on his frame. "Stocky, red-faced and cigar smoking, looking more like a longshoreman than the chief state school officer of the Commonwealth," was the way The New Bedford Standard Times once portrayed him.

A Wax Museum-like caricature of him might have included the head of Theodore Roosevelt atop the torso of Winston Churchill. The only major deviation from this lofty combination would have been the continuous presence of "a big grin, a chuckle and a red, red face." This was how a long-time Boston Globe reporter remembered the first impression Anrig made on her (Cohen 1994).

Another characterization of the sort that belied Anrig's educational and professional background came from Frank Keppel, a respected educational leader of the mid-twentieth century. As a postscript to a letter recommending Anrig for the post of President of the Educational Testing Service, he wrote: "You may be surprised by the first appearance; his beaming face and rotund figure makes one think of one's favorite bartender. He is in fact a sober and serious man" (Keppel 1980).

When Anrig entered a room full of people he filled it as much with his expansive smile and solid gait as with his sheer width. Although not much for social touching, like hugging and cheek kissing, he relished shaking people's hands. And when he shook a hand, especially for the first time, the owner tended not to forget it.

He was nearly always animated – in public, perpetually mixing jocularity with an air of purposiveness, forever exhibiting a friendly boisterousness backed by an undercurrent of seriousness. In younger years this aura must have prompted some of his school teachers to wonder if he was engaged in mischief behind the "scene" he was busy creating around himself. One close colleague and mentor recalled the overall effect aptly as that of a "perambulatory hurricane" (Howe 1994).

Not only did he fill space in a room in proportion to his dimensions and demeanor, he somehow managed to fill others' space as well. He never did this in an offensive, demanding, intrusive or threatening way, but rather, artfully, benevolently inviting those around him to a place outside themselves where they might be allowed the luxury of less fear.

Andrea Ossip, who had been in his homeroom class at Eastview Junior High School in White Plains in the mid-fifties, plainly reinforces this point. "Red" (the nickname the kids used for him) was her homeroom teacher for three years. "In that time I never had him for a class," she said, " but he managed to give me a sense of its being OK to be me. He made me feel safe. He treated me with respect, humor and seriousness." Finally she noted that even though she had seen him only occasionally over the years since Eastview, she was continually impressed with the way "he made a space for me in his heart" (Ossip 1994).

In more intimate professional meetings, conferring across a desk or table, he was more relaxed than in a large public meeting. He was no less animated though, just more internal, less outer-directed. A good deal of the time he was pensive and serious, with his shoulders almost always thrust forward to talk, gesture or listen. It was as if he was intuitively able to adjust the magnitude of his presence to the size of the room in which he was working, as well as to the assertiveness or lack thereof on the part of his guests.

Except in the most serious of circumstances his volubility was a fixture at meetings he attended or ran. But this verbal amiability was always set off against a deep current of self-containment. To fellow conversants at the table he openly but quietly offered some of his plentiful personal force. Yet he held back most of it, unintentionally perhaps capturing more of the total that was available in the space in which he was working.

Anrig's power stemmed not only from his presence, but from his perspicacity, his prescience - a set of special abilities to glean from complex circumstances their essential meaning for both the present and the future. In fact, somewhere in between these latter two, perspicacity and prescience, was the way his mind worked. In any given discussion he seemed to be the one who saw through ideas and circumstances to their quick. He focused narrowly on the central element amidst an array of distractions and then articulated the essential issue and possible next moves.

In a classic sense he was a strategist inspired by vision and values rather than a poet inspired by a muse or a scientist questing for discovery. His mind was much more oriented to dealing with near term applications, in all instances shaped by enduring values and long term vision. If the whole point of scientific inquiry is to allow no bar to continuous debate, Anrig eschewed science. While he promoted, and very much enjoyed, vigorous debate, he needed and demanded closure. When it was achieved, he relished moving on as opposed to going over old ground. This meant that he was superb at tactical maneuvering, not so good at tracing new lines of inquiry within a broad framework of ideas.

The act that often represented the crest of his intellectual contribution to a discussion was his delineating with great rapidity necessary next steps: ". . . first we might want to do this and then that, then together we might consider this other thing, followed by something a little off beat that might work too, and to make a real difference it would be a good idea if we . . . ."

His own phrase for all of the above was the "squinty-eyed view". But like so many of his other mildly self-deprecating formulations, it was much too modest. There was a lot more going on than just focusing in on priorities amidst a confusing array of phenomena. His mind rapidly generated and carefully stored a broad range of options and opportunities. Then he quickly selected the ones with most promise for the given situation, and issued them one after the other in a sensible order of priority. Red Hill, head of the Massachusetts School Superintendents' Association, captured the kinetics if not the dynamics of this behavior quite accurately, by calling Anrig "a duck on water – calm on the surface, but paddling like hell underneath" (Pave 1981). This image of web feet sequentially pushing water aside to get to sustenance, sun or shade characterizes accurately the way he conducted himself in professional situations.

As with so many other leaders, Anrig worked hard to refine his considerable innate abilities. Over the course of his professional career he put extraordinary effort into expanding the portfolio of "free advice" he offered so openly to all wise enough to ask. One of his ETS Board members, Alan "Scotty" Campbell, recalls with awe that he was seemingly never unprepared for interactions with his Board, whether a full-blown decision making discussion or a one-on-one with a Board member (Campbell 1994). A noted ETS research scientist, Sam Messick, commented that Anrig had become reasonably adept at psychometrics (the science of taking mental measurements through testing) toward the end of his Presidency. He had known very little about the field when he started. Messick attributed this turn as much to Anrig's intellectual grit and stick-to-itiveness as to his innate brightness (Messick 1994).

If forced to describe his genius at interpersonal interactions as a series of sequential steps, I would suggest that the list would include at least these elements. He would start off a group conversation with a patch of self-deprecatory humor - to communicate that he saw himself as much of a flawed human as any in the room. This move would usually encourage most in the room to relax, at least a little bit. Next, if it was a meeting he was leading, he would announce an agenda, not in a particularly assertive fashion, but rather almost matter-of-factly. This was not only to get on with business, but to demonstrate that he was neither withholding essential information nor bent on plying hidden agendas.

As he announced the topics for consideration, he also found a way of declaring one of his most abiding values, that no matter where the discussion led or how hot it got, no one had to worry about losing a whit of personal dignity. Usually he managed to achieve this latter effect with body language and an anecdote of some sort. A joking reference to how some clerical workers who were picketing the Department of Education offices had reacted to his serving them coffee during a mid-winter strike would serve such a purpose.

When all these preliminaries were over it was time to get down to the serious business at hand. Almost always Anrig would find a way, no matter what the actual topic, to bring into the discussion one or more of his core concerns such as the centrality of teaching and learning or fair treatment for all.

Whether in charge of the discussion or not, he would also find a way to ensure that the session end with some sort of closure, either a listing of next steps or a rendering of continuing challenges.

Anrig demonstrated unusual attributes like the ones just described in a variety of situations and circumstances. Those he may be best known for settle within the frame of the four major public policy issues identified in the Introduction: the centrality of teaching and learning, equality of educational opportunity; the shaping of state, local and federal roles in relation to each other; and the character of educational assessment.

His work on these issues was, as we will see later, revealing of his leadership capacities. But the way in which he handled the direction of his own professional life was most reflective of the character that underlay those capacities. When it was his future, his livelihood and the well being of his family that were on the line, he showed his leadership core.

He decided "against the grain" to go to Washington to serve the cause of educational innovation and civil rights in the mid-60's; he chose state service in the 70's because he alone believed "that's where the action will be"; and he joined ETS in the 80's just as widespread national concern for educational quality and how to measure it reached a new high water mark.

These career junctures were both summative and instructive. They reflected great deliberativeness and real insight into the social context in which he was operating. Moreover, they indicated rather phenomenal anticipation of moments in which matters of national import were coming to the fore of public consideration. Ultimately they displayed a unique one-to-one relationship between his decision making about his own being and the decision making he did on behalf of others. What he did for himself - to join fully with issues of social consequence - he saw as his duty to do for others.

There was yet another major facet of Anrig's force beyond his mental scope and capacity, beyond even the character reflected in the kind of decision making he did with regard to his own career development. It is a condition of being that transcends any particular set of situations, issues or decisions. Simply put, Anrig's actions aligned more closely with his values than almost all of his fellow human beings.   The assertion of Nancy Cole, his successor at ETS, warrants mention here. She said, "The gap between Greg's stated values and his actions was smaller than any person I have ever known" (Cole 1994).

This condition, of near total coincidence between values and actions, was invaluable to him as a public affairs leader. It made his behavior eminently predictable, from one set of circumstances to the next, one audience to the next, one time frame to the next. All one had to do was listen carefully to what he said he was about or what he said he was going to do. It was something upon which others could rely. So even if one did not agree with him or like him, one had to respect his words - a fairly rare situation in contemporary public affairs.

How closely his actions and values coincided is reflected in the subtleties of one interchange recorded from the interviews conducted for this book. The turns in the interchange may be a bit startling, but they show great consonance between what he valued and what he did. Early in his tenure as ETS President, Anrig appointed an internal committee made up of a cross section of staff to give him unfiltered advice on issues affecting their work life in the organization. This was a controversial and somewhat unprecedented move since the group reported directly to him even though most of its members reported to other officers in the organization for the bulk of their assignments.

When the term of the current committee chair expired, Anrig inquired of this person if he would be willing to continue for an additional term. He arrived at Anrig's office to discuss the matter, and demurred politely from the offer. He explained that the way ETS had responded to some of his own family difficulties would likely result in his decision to bring suit against ETS to recover educational expenses he did not believe were his responsibility. It would in his view be awkward for Anrig to reenlist a person as chair of a personnel-oriented group who was suing the organization on a personnel-related matter.

Anrig listened to all this and responded matter-of-factly that he fully expected the committee chair to act with his family interests topmost in mind. But actions taken on behalf of his family were really unrelated to his original request that the man continue as chair. This last sentence of Anrig's response was actually tacit, offered through body language rather than words. The committee chair was left to wonder for a few seconds if indeed "the other shoe had dropped" and he was being asked to step down rather than step up to the chairpersonship.

Quietly yet vigorously Anrig reaffirmed his request that the person continue as chair, brushing aside other matters he considered extraneous. However unexpected it was for the person who initiated the conversation, this was the outcome. It arrived after little back and forth, no questions asked, no points elaborated, no hemming and hawing - all of which might have been more normal. Anrig in fact treated the outcome as a given. To the receiver it felt more like a special gift, a powerful form of reinforcement offered up even more powerfully because it remained implicit rather than explicit.

More often than not in our organizational lives we have been on the receiving end of a markedly different approach to our personal and professional quandaries. More likely responses are these. "It really would look bad." "We need to think more about this." "I'm totally behind you, and I really appreciate your great service, but. . . . " Traditional organizational norms had led the committee chair to expect that the opposite message was about to be proffered, and when it wasn't, the effect was memorable.

As this story demonstrates, at the top of Anrig's exceedingly short list of values was a premium on preserving other people's dignity, by first and foremost acknowledging their integrity. For him this took the form of a lived discipline of reciprocity, treating other people as you wished to be treated, a daily commitment to struggle to see things from the other person's perspective, to live in the other person's shoes. Rhoda Schneider, an attorney who worked with Anrig at the Massachusetts Department of Education, recalled in a letter, "I remember hearing you on a radio call-in show, when you had to field a question that was a thinly veiled diatribe against desegregation. I was so struck by the respect and kindness with which you treated the caller, even while pointedly refuting his thesis" (Schneider 1994).

Equally convincing on this same point, Muriel Cohen, a hard-nosed reporter who covered education for the <u>Boston Globe</u> when Anrig was Massachusetts Commissioner, recalls the following situation. He had invited her to attend a national conference on assessment after he had left Massachusetts state service and gone to ETS. She noted parenthetically that he had kept in pretty frequent contact with her after his departure even though she only occasionally covered the national education scene.

She arrived at the conference and went to the first general session where she saw Anrig talking to several people at another table. She approached him, but was kept at bay by someone who appeared to be his public relations aide. Later on in the day she finally made contact with him in the hall and told him what had happened earlier. He was incensed, apologized over and over again to her, assuring her that it would never happen again. The heart-to-heart discussion he likely had with the aide was probably restrained, but left little doubt of his predilections on matters of this sort (Cohen 1994).

Second on the short list of his values was a deep commitment to helping others. He believed that citizenship meant a fair sharing of available opportunities through persistent service to one's fellow human beings. Here is what he said in a talk he gave upon receiving a special award from the high school he attended:

- We are put on this earth not just to serve our own needs;
- Helping others can be wonderfully fulfilling, personally and professionally;
- To the extent you are blessed with any talent or opportunity, with that blessing comes an obligation to give back to others what that talent or opportunity has made possible for you;
- You should stand for something, and one of these commitments ought to be to help those who have not been as fortunate in their lives as you have;
- Helping people get a good education and a fair break in life can be a doorway of opportunity for them and fulfilling for you. (Anrig 1987)

According to Martha Zeigler, advocate for the educational rights of disabled children when Anrig served as Commissioner, his commitment to equality of educational opportunity went well beyond allegiance to the principle. He had a "deep concern for children as individuals," she said. "He did not want anybody to be left out" (Zeigler 1994).

As Education Commissioner he repeatedly demonstrated this commitment to helping others while at the same time holding firmly to values. One case in point involved a state legislator who sought to dissuade him from taking a particular position on a policy issue. In a conversation in his office, Anrig and the legislator aired their disagreement, but were not able to overcome it. As the tussling was winding down and the talk turned to less volatile topics, the legislator let slip that he had not been able to secure appropriate educational services for his handicapped child.

Subsequent to the meeting Anrig personally intervened with local officials to assist the legislator with his quandary as a parent. At the same time he steadfastly refused to budge on his divergent position on the policy matter that had brought them together in the first place. According to Mike Daly, Anrig's deputy, who witnessed these events and had subsequent contact with the legislator, the latter never forgot the experience. He had failed to secure politically what he approached an agency head for, but had received personally far more than he had ever expected (Daly 1994).

Anrig's basic values were an interesting mix of liberalism and conservatism. When assembled in one set, they tended to look a lot like those of an early American patriot submitting reluctantly to late 20th Century social trends. As an illustration, he had great difficulty with the concept of abortion, as noted by a close Massachusetts ally of his, Sandra Lynch. He could not imagine any person not wanting a child and acting on that negative inclination. He also had related concerns about the redefinition of women's roles as they were developing in the mid-seventies. Personally he was more comfortable with the traditional definition than with the emerging one. What made the ultimate difference for him, however, was that he valued individual freedom and elemental fairness above other considerations. He therefore not only came to grasp the emerging redefinition, but also was able to act on it professionally. Eventually he even embraced it, personally as well as professionally (Lynch 1994).

While honoring the warrants of individual freedom, Anrig nonetheless stood by the idea that freedom was inseparable from responsibility. The essence of what he valued was freedom and fairness for the individual bounded by the robust responsibilities of citizenship. These were the very dimensions he outlined in the speech at the high school where, as a youth, he likely learned to think them and act them out.

Third, in this short list of his values, was an airtight commitment to family - to the mutual support and love that comes from its cohesion. The nuclear family in which he grew up was not the model he invented with his wife, Charlotte. That earlier family was scarred with the premature death of a father and a mother who, because of financial constraint, had to depend on others to help raise two boys, his brother and himself.

Perhaps the disruption that had been visited on him as a child reinforced his commitment to family as untouchable sacred ground. In any case, the closeness and deep loyalties that characterized the family Charlotte and he put together were especially noteworthy given the "script" of the family in which he had grown up. Anrig's achievements as the head of a family cut strongly against the grain of "repeat performance" from generation to generation that we have come to expect as the norm in the present social context.

The mateship that formed between Charlotte and him was on the surface a traditional one. He was the breadwinner and she the homemaker for the most part. Below the surface, however, there were other more unusual facets. On all fronts, he trusted and depended on her judgment and her balance. In fact, were it not for the personal foundation of support she provided, I believe the professional contributions he made would not have been possible. She was the builder and custodian of the foundation, he the architect and craftsman responsible for much of the visible, above ground structure.

His family bonds were so riveting that they occasionally caused some anomalous behavior on his part. Almost nothing could get him more riled than an act that did harm to one of his nuclear family. At one point in his early adulthood, his oldest son precipitously lost an opportunity he had worked a year to nurture. He had secured a book contract and had done all the background research for an in-depth study of a major media organization. The organization's leaders had provided consistent support to the effort. Then, in what seemed to be a spasm of last-minute paranoiac jitters, top management pulled the plug and a year's work went down the drain. The older Anrig "lost his cool." He telephoned several at the organization and demanded an explanation. One of those who received a call said she had never heard him so angry (Cohen 1994).

There were a few people beyond his nuclear family that he treated as if they were family. These individuals were accorded the same access to his protectiveness as were the members of his own family. They were also among a very small number that saw some of the vulnerability that he rarely showed in public. I was fortunate enough to be among that small number.

The preservation of the elemental personal dignity and worth of all he met and worked with, an active and robust brand of citizenship, and the protection of the welfare of those closest to him - these were his most deeply held values. Two others, honesty and perseverance, complement these three. They give even more force and meaning to the brand of leadership Anrig demonstrated.

His honesty grew from a clear sense of who he was as a person and a thoroughgoing commitment to a "no bones" approach to the public presentation of his persona. He therefore had little patience with various forms of social dissimulation, what we refer to today in the vernacular as "game playing." He much preferred authenticity even when it took the form of outright racism or other forms of social pathology. It was not as if he lacked social graces. Quite the contrary, many who observed him over the years in social situations were taken by his amiable and cheerful presence. In fact they would show mild surprise at his perpetual absence from academic cocktail parties or similar events where people display more ego than empathy.

There was another piece of reinforcement for Anrig's honesty. It came quite simply from his belief that honest dealings in public affairs produced the greatest degree of effectiveness. If you wanted to get something done, honesty was almost always the best policy. This was true even if it caused pain. As Janet Bowker who worked with him at ETS said, "It was more important to Anrig to be honest than to absorb personal damage" (Bowker 1994).

In his work life, he appreciated dealing with others who were as honest about themselves as he was. Almost as much he appreciated those who exhibited great effort and showed unusual capacity to stick with a task to completion. He himself had a disproportionate commitment to "pushing elephants up hills." And he enjoyed seeing colleagues display similar tendencies. When those around him showed signs of wanting to "pack it in" for the evening after a long and frustrating day, he would press on, maintaining the same intellectual grasp he had at the beginning of the day. He seemed determined to keep at it until there was some closure, some progress, some sense that it would be possible to generate and keep momentum on an issue of consequence.

His Board at ETS thought he worked too hard, and they were probably right. Although pure speculation, it is possible to attribute his early death, at age 63, to the constant pounding he chose to absorb for the sake of fulfillment of mission, the completion of task. The one thing that was true is that he loved hard work, especially work that entailed wrestling with complex social issues, where, if a solution could be found, some class of deserving citizens might benefit.

One way to grasp the essentials of Anrig's character as public affairs leader is through the economy of the four words whose meaning has already been plumbed in this chapter: presence, perspicacity or prescience, predictability and perseverance. Together they form a simple, almost linear, backdrop for the whole landscape as well as the most prominent points of his professional work and contributions. He was indeed able to see through complex circumstances (perspicacity), even to the extent of more than occasionally seeing what was on the other side (prescience). Yet he never lost the ability to stand in the present and deal effectively in person with the multiple demands of a social context, ethical and political intertwined (presence).

Throughout, he exhibited a disciplined consistency between actions and values (predictability) that engendered admiration in those who knew him well and a slight bewilderment in those who did not, wondering if indeed a person could be that transparent. Finally he adhered repeatedly to those values (perseverance), relying on them over and over in new contexts and different circumstances. He was rarely deterred. Even if momentarily deflected, he always returned to the fray fresh and full of humor the day following the one in which he had just taken a beating.

Another slightly more professional sounding yet simpler encapsulation of his considerable capacities is as follows. Anrig managed simultaneously to be a very effective "retailer of good will" in the public forum, as well as a brilliant, or at least highly capable, "systems designer and engineer." This is to say, he brought together very different capacities necessary for effective leadership in complex organizations and political contexts.

He had three key assets. First was a real knack for putting people at ease in all the social situations in which he was doing business. Second was a mind like a tempered steel blade when it came to shaping policy. Third was a will of iron in the context of making moves on behalf of organizational effectiveness. Softening the social edges in difficult situations while being incisive about aim and purpose and in addition having the will and wherewithal to get things done in complex organizational environments - these make for a powerful mix for someone seeking to play a lead role in public affairs.

Chapter 3

Educational Leadership Headwaters

> *"The river, surging course,*
> *Uninterrupted current.*
> *Headwater, channel, mouth.*
> *Can they be divided?"*
>
> *Deng Ming-Dao 1992, #15*

"If you hear a quiet classroom suddenly break into laughter, you know someone there in that room is Greg Anrig."- *an excerpt from The Echo, Tenafly High School Newspaper, 1949.*

The River of a Life

Writing about Anrig's life may be like stitching together pieces of a quilt, but the metaphor does nothing to capture what the living of his life must have been like for him. His professional life was probably more like a confluence of streams emerging as a powerful river.

Rivulets of commitment appeared early and gained strength in his youth. Principal among these were the key role of schooling in a person's development, the central place of teaching and learning in schooling, and the imperative of ensuring a fair shake for those of little means or disadvantage. For the young Anrig these were not remote abstractions like "starving millions in Asia." Rather they were ideas that sustained him through some of his own hard times growing up.

In the early stages of his career these rivulets flowed together into a more powerful stream of concern for equality of educational opportunity. What had begun as a youthful commitment to a "fair shake" for everybody became transformed in his mid-thirties into a life-consuming preoccupation with the promise of changes in national policy. The aim of these changes was to guarantee equal access for all to an education of quality.

Then in his forties another tributary joined the expanding channel. It was the conviction that the state, in careful balance with the federal government and local districts, could collect and deploy powerful positive energy for better teaching and learning and fair access of all people to these invaluable assets. This channel ran deeper inside him because he had learned, first as student and then teacher and later as architect of teacher development programs, that educational policies were only as effective as the teachers that executed them. The classroom was the sole true crucible of educational policy.

All the flow that preceded came together in his fifties in the perceived potential of assessment to serve improved instruction and to advance equitable treatment of all students. None of the hydraulic force of his prior efforts on behalf of equal access or the promise of the state role was lost as the water of his life moved downstream. It served only to increase the depth and expand the breadth of the river as it cut its way to the sea.

As noted in "Leadership Character", Anrig turned in each of his last three or four career moves to a venue that was about to become a major political battleground. First was the federal government arena in the sixties where there was an abundant sense of mission and much momentum for social change. Then a troubled city and lighthouse state in the 70's where authority figures and ordinary citizens faced off against each other and in the process intensified the nation's most difficult social challenge. Finally the riveting domain of testing where individual aspiration meets coarsely calibrated judgment, rendered results frequently sting, and allegations of unfairness abound.

The river that eventually became Anrig's life was fed in formative years by history teaching, an initial venture into school administration as an assistant principal, then a principalship followed by a rural superintendency. After tracking such a relatively predictable contour line of educational leadership, the river shifted course. It established a new direction, became broader and deeper, and ran through reaches of terrain that offered a more expansive view. This change began with his service in 1967 with the U.S. Office of Education's Division of Equal Educational Opportunity. It continued when he left federal service and became involved in designing and implementing a new kind of a school of education at the Boston Campus of the University of Massachusetts.

The banks of the river widened and deepened again and its pace increased dramatically during his time at the Massachusetts Department of Education. He became State Commissioner a year before a Federal Judge ruled in favor of Black plaintiffs in a major desegregation case, whereupon substantial turbulence overcame the schools and neighborhoods of a socially divided city - and a year after the state enacted the nation's first comprehensive measure on educating disabled students.

The flow crested when he assumed the Presidency of the Educational Testing Service in 1981. He undertook this role as truth-in-testing advocates vociferously held forth in legislative and congressional hearings; as the media used the grist that advocates had provided to blast the testing establishment; as the U.S. Secretary of Education undertook to publish his first "Wall Chart" comparing states on existing test score data; and as elected officials in almost all states began setting education policy grounded in greater accountability of teachers, schools and districts.

Beginning in the mid-sixties Anrig became visible and active at important "teachable moments" for American society. As the following chapters show, he took this course because he believed he had a responsibility to contribute as a citizen leader. Whatever the challenges of a particular assignment, he plied an agenda that was based on values to which he had become committed early on in his life. These were his persistent compass bearings. In each successive role the opportunities to serve multiplied, the issues became more complex and intertwined, and the pace of action more rapid and intense.

His life was indeed like a river. Its depth and breadth increased as it traversed the land through which it coursed. Like a river it gained in magnitude from joining tributaries and smaller streams. And at times, like a river, his life swelled against its own banks and even exceeded them. Its hydraulic, or force of flow, grew as it moved on. And like a river his life nourished and at the same time altered the character of the terrain through which it coursed. Like a river his ultimate destination was suffusion with the larger body that nourishes us, the ocean of our collective consciousness.

Early Years

What were the headwaters of this river of Anrig's life? What kind of persons and circumstances spawned him? Where did he originate and who and what made a difference to him as he was getting his start in life? Gregory Richard Anrig was reared in less than felicitous circumstances. If viewed solely from the frame of his nuclear family, his was a childhood in distress. His father died when he was three. His mother, finding it difficult to cope with the economic challenges of single parenting, sought alternative living arrangements for both him and his older brother Raymond while they were still very young.

The family's ethnic background was a mix of mostly Irish on his mother's side and mostly Swiss on his father's. At one point, later in his life when he had achieved some name recognition, a woman wrote him out of the blue asking if he was related to the Anrig family that had been prominent in a particular village in Switzerland. Anrig graciously wrote back to her, suggesting she might be on target, but referring her to someone else in the family who would likely be more interested in family roots and origins.

At six the youngest Anrig was sent to a residential military school. Then for the next few years he lived with his grandparents in New York City. Beginning in early adolescence he boarded with families in his original hometown of Tenafly, New Jersey. These "foster home" arrangements spanned all of his high school years. They did as well for his older sibling, Raymond. During this period of almost a decade, his mother resided and earned a living as a secretary in New York City, over an hour's ride away from Tenafly. Even while he was in elementary school, he frequently rode the bus on the weekends to visit her across the Hudson River in her Manhattan apartment.

This pattern, of reaching out to his mother even as she remained at a distance, prevailed for his entire life. Through most of her later years, he took nearly sole responsibility for her maintenance and care. As it turned out, she managed to outlive him. At the writing of this text she is over ninety and lives in a nursing home in New Jersey. Through financial resources he left behind, her care is assured through the end of her life (Charlotte Anrig 1994).

His own commentary on his upbringing, offered several decades later, provides some useful insight:

> I had a strange existence as a child, including a year in military school and several years living with my grandparents in New York City before boarding with three families. A lot of kids in that situation could have gone off the deep end. (Pave 1981)

In seeking to understand how Anrig managed not to "go off the deep end" in his youth, how on the contrary he transcended his less than promising "script", the perspective of a noted psychotherapist comes in handy. He said of childhood:

> There is, in fact, an aspect of the child that is utterly exposed to fate, time and conditions - not protected by being in a more personal context. Yet this exposure is what allows the child to become someone new and powerful. (Moore 1992, 50)

This is exactly what happened in Anrig's case. He drew from the systems around him what he needed to survive, and beyond that, to thrive. Very early on in his school career he grew to rely on the support that school could provide. School became an "anchor to windward" in a way that it might not have for another child. In his own words:

> I was one of those strange kids who loved school -- not the homework and the tests, of course, but the kids and teachers and all the activities (even the legitimate ones). Life at school meant a lot to me, and I enjoyed it to the fullest each day.   (Anrig 1987)

Listen to these recollections, ones that he himself collected for a talk he made in 1987 when he was honored as the outstanding graduate of Tenafly High School:

> I remember "Griff", our wonderful music director. He tolerated my trombone playing and horseplay. He taught me perseverance, discipline and responsibility.
>
> I remember "Missy" Hargraves, a wonderfully sensitive social studies teacher. She loved history, but she loved her students even more. She would calmly respond to the most ridiculous antic with an "Oh, Greg, you're at it again." . . . I majored in history and became a social studies teacher because of Miss Hargrave's inspiration.
>
> I remember Miss Dower, our 12th grade English teacher. Miss Dower believed that the paragraph was literature! There were only two grades you could get for a paragraph in Miss Dower's class -- an "A" or an "F". Along with you I growled at the unfairness of this. But today, every time I write I thank my lucky stars that I had Miss Dower for English. I can still write a good paragraph.
>
> I remember "warming the bench" on the football team. Coach Clark put me in once for a kickoff. The ball was received by an All-State fullback for Teaneck. Of all the luck, he headed for   me. To this day I can't remember what happened. The bench was safer.
>
> I remember having a part in the musical "Desert Song." Left on the stage by myself I was to bend to one knee and sing a song to a balcony off stage left where my love was soon to be.   When I started to sing to my "love" on opening night, there on the catwalk off stage and above were my friends, Mike, Howie and "Smitty" looking down and making faces at me. That is when I learned self-control!
>
> I remember Coach Yockers getting even with me for breaking training on the track team by entering me in the half-mile race. I had never even walked a half-mile much less run one. That is where I learned the meaning of misery.

I remember Miss Pokorney, my algebra teacher, good naturedly answering my daily question, "What good will algebra ever be to me in the future?" She used to keep me after school, until I started practicing my trombone in her room at the end of the day. (I should have thought of that one sooner!)

I remember wonderful girlfriends and dances and parties, but those are memories I will recall only with classmates. After all, my mother and dear wife are here in the audience. (Anrig 1987)

Indeed it was a touch of Victorian propriety that prevented him from remembering out loud at this award ceremony in front of his wife and mother that his first date was with Joan Bell. She took him to a barn dance. And, along with Mike Bryson, he took Joan Alber and Ruthie Finck on an excursion to New York City for dinner and a show. It is unclear from the scant reports in The Echo, the high school newspaper, exactly who paired off with whom, and it probably matters little at this point (The Echo 1949).

There were other positive influences on his life beyond the adults who shepherded him in school - and the young women who accompanied him to social events. Fortunately for him, he spent a number of productive and satisfying summers at a church camp for youth in Connecticut called Camp Pequot. The camp director took a deep interest in his personal development. That interest and the youthful Anrig's responsiveness resulted eventually in his ascendancy to the role of counselor, an assignment he repeated for almost ten summers. The "experience," as he pondered it later in life, "convinced me I wanted to work with young people. I needed them and they needed me. It gave me a sense of importance" (Pave 1981).

His repeated summers as a camp counselor also provided him with the opportunity to meet his future wife, Charlotte. They met in a bar where they were both out relaxing one summer evening in Ivoryton, Connecticut. She was a young Kindergarten teacher in Deep River, Connecticut, where she had been brought up. This was not far from Camp Pequot where Anrig worked as counselor. After a courtship of one year, they were married in a small church in Deep River. Eventually they had three children. The oldest, Greg, Jr., is presently a policy analyst/writer, working for the Twentieth Century Fund in New York City. The middle child, Susan, is a teacher in a Manhattan public elementary school. The youngest, Chris, works as a private school teacher in New Jersey. All three are married.

In a gesture that captured well the nature of their common inclinations, Charlotte invited her entire Kindergarten class to their wedding in June, 1957. The youngsters not only showed up in force, but immediately following the ceremony, Charlotte went around to each of them to shake their hands and thank them for coming.

With the formalities concluded, the bride and groom prepared to leave. The car they were to take was outside the church. Politely the groom opened the passenger door so the bride could get in. When she was comfortably seated, he nestled in beside her on the same side. But there was no additional person to drive them. Quickly he sensed his *faut pas,* jumped from the passenger seat and ran around to the other side, his face as red as a rose petal (Anrig, Charlotte 1994).

There is much to ponder in all these tales. First off is the powerfully sympathetic support many of those around him provided. It began with his school teachers and administrators and camp leaders. It became even more profoundly the case with the person he chose to be around the rest of his life. She became his major backstop, his primary support system throughout his career.

He recounted at the Tenafly award ceremony an array of humorous situations. In most he portrayed himself as the perpetual "n'ere do well." Collectively, the stories serve as superficial cloak at best for the great regard in which he held the school professionals who helped him learn and grow. They were indeed his best friends. Most fortunately for him, this was exactly the dynamic that characterized the relationship he and Charlotte built. He frequently referred to her as his best friend. In one newspaper interview he amplified the point, noting that she "is a great judge of my moods. She says that when my face gets red, you know I"m angry. When it turns white, it's time to take the kids and get out of the house" (Pave 1981).

Behind almost all the recollections is a powerful theme. Anrig was not only determined but intuitively very able to get what he needed, not in any material sense particularly, but rather emotionally and spiritually. He had an unusual capacity for managing the people around him for the sake of his own growth. At the same time he was able to fulfill what others were asking of him, and more than occasionally add to their joy and even their own growth. He was, it seemed, very clearheaded about what all these people could offer him, from his early charges at Camp Pequot to his closest ally, Charlotte.

In completing the brief questionnaire the Tenafly Schools sent him in anticipation of his receiving their award, he reinforces this very impression. Referring to his living with other families he commented:

> Because of this unusual living arrangement, school -- especially high school -- was the center of my life. My horsing around with friends and teachers really was a way to "soak up" during school hours the human interaction that others enjoyed during all their waking hours. Thankfully, my teachers (and most of the time, my principal) understood this. They were friends as well as instructors. (Anrig 1987)

"Retailer of good will" combined with "systems designer or engineer" were the metaphors I used at the end of "Leadership Character" to describe his unusual capacities. Not surprisingly, both show through in his formative experiences in Tenafly. One can discern from his own recollections and others' commentary how the two capacities joined forces in the mindset he developed to deal with the world. Through relatively innocent playfulness and robust humor he spread good will among the significant adults, youthful peers and younger children in his life. Simultaneously he very skillfully organized around himself a great array of helpful arrangements and activities to advance the legitimate cause of his own personal development.

That Anrig did not confine the application of these considerable capacities to his school and camp life makes this contention about him even more applicable. One of the children from the family with which he boarded in high school - now over sixty - observed as follows. He said his mother, Mrs. Goodyear, exerted a marked influence on the young Anrig. Like him, she was very interested in literature. For sustained periods nearly every day after school, the young boarder and Mrs. Goodyear would converse about what he was reading and how he might interpret it and better glean its meaning. It appears then as if Anrig did the same in his adopted homes as he did in school and at camp: he found a way to get what he needed and thereby thrive, rather than withdraw in face of the absence of his biological parents.

It must though have been extraordinarily difficult to spend almost all of one's time growing up in other people's spaces, not one's own. For example, the adult Anrig often attributed his persistent overweight to the fact that as a child he rarely had free access to the refrigerator in the house in which he was living (Author's Recollection). So when he became autonomous, he resolved to make up for the deficiency. This he managed to do most admirably and amply! He altered many attitudes and habits as he grew, but a poor diet stuck with him throughout his life. All - both family and friends - who attempted to persuade him of the merits and benefits of responsible eating repeatedly failed in the face of his earnest conviction to the contrary.

On the plus side, as already noted, his early positioning as outsider thrust inside other people's nuclear families caused him to perfect a relaxed and amiable mien. This well-shaped and robust diplomacy served him well throughout his professional life. It also occasionally raised some eyebrows. For example, one ETS colleague who professed great respect for him, said that he believed that Anrig might have harbored some shame-ridden, secret life that no one at the office ever saw. This colleague noted his impression that "the closer you got to him the more unknowable he was" (Ramsey 1994).

Whether he had big closeted secrets is unverifiable, even in this People Magazine era of ours. But it is highly unlikely given the conditions of his latency and adolescence. What was unusual about him was that the private space he kept for himself, while no less firmly held than others, was relatively more confined. This was the adaptation he made to traverse successfully the challenges of his early years, and that which led in all likelihood to impressions like the one his ETS colleague formed.

Ironically, part of the truth of his "unknowability" is that it was virtually non-existent. For the currents of his public persona ran deeper and extended wider than most people's. On this very point his youngest son offered an interesting observation. His father, he said, seemed able to infuse all his social interactions with the best of what he had learned from his early interactions with ad hoc family members - teachers, foster parents and camp leaders. He made frequent references to them for the benefit of his own children (Anrig, Chris 1994).

Another ETS colleague, Bob Solomon, recalling how Anrig conducted himself as President, noted that his leadership actions infused his "every waking moment." "Greg", he said, "was a thoroughgoing 'leadership performer' as opposed to the more frequently seen 'leadership part-player'." In light of the fact that so much of his personal being was "professionalized" during his formative years, the statement is hardly a surprising one. His early growth and development depended on his honing unusual interpersonal skills; that they maintained a steady and pervasive hold on all facets of his later life might be seen as inevitable.

For Anrig this unique merging of the personal and the professional - like the merging of two streams coming together - became his abiding inner context. It was the singular integrated way he viewed all of life, the central means through which he acted upon his environment. It explains in significant part his exquisite contributions to the field of public affairs leadership.

Chapter 4

Attending to Civil Rights

"Those of you here today may feel that these concerns (racial segregation) are remote from your own. They are not. During three years in Washington I had the chance to work with a large number of Southern communities. It has been interesting to me to observe the progress that has taken place in the South once community leadership faced up to the issue of racial segregation. In cities and towns across the former Confederacy, there seems to be a rebirth of vigor in public policy and a resurgence of economic vitality. As demagoguery has faded a new brand of progressive leadership has appeared at the local and state levels. One dramatic result has been an economic reawakening across the South. This bodes well for the future. I believe the South has a chance to surpass the North as a place to live, to learn and to work. This is important to you whose firms have a stake in the future of this city." From a speech Anrig made to the Boston Rotary Club in 1973, "Education in Boston - Past, Present and Future." (Anrig 1973)

The Essence of the Topic

For Americans civil rights are universal entitlements. They are what we are owed because we set foot on the earth.

Among other things, they provide for equal starting places for us all. When we are secure in our civil rights, we can conduct our lives with the same legal standing as our fellow human beings. Because of these rights we are all supposed to have an equal opportunity to achieve full social and economic benefits. To attend to civil rights means to spend one's days seeing after them, being sure that they become a real part of the social fabric, and that once they infuse people's lives, they are cared for remain in place for good.

Anrig spent three decades of his life attending to civil rights. More than any other issue this one was dominant for him. Were I to chronicle every major action that made up his civil rights portfolio, the final product would be a bulging compendium. Were I to trace the evolution of his thinking on the matter, more than one book length piece would emerge. This chapter, while it may not do full justice to a thirty-year career in civil rights, includes the key elements and conveys the essence of the story. It provides a sense of the breadth, depth, direction and flow of this main channel of the river of his life.

Starting in Earnest with Three Years in Washington

In 1965 the President proposed and Congress enacted the Elementary and Secondary Education Act (ESEA), the largest package of general education aid passed up to that time to serve primarily the needs of poor children. A year before, the same two branches of government had joined forces to bring into law the Civil Rights Act (CRA). It warranted, among other things, that states and localities move affirmatively to desegregate their schools. In so doing they would become eligible for federal aid. In effect, by the late sixties, the resources of the ESEA were positioned to meet the thrust of the CRA head on. The money was there as aid for poor children's schooling, but it had the tight strings of civil rights compliance attached.

At the crossroads of the brewing controversies generated by the conjunction of these forces was Harold "Doc"

Howe II, the U.S. Commissioner of Education. His boss, John Gardner, Secretary of Health, Education and Welfare, had with Howe's concurrence just decided to place responsibility for the legal enforcement of the Civil Rights Act in the HEW Secretary's office. This left to the Office of Education, which Howe headed, the all important task of helping school districts that were out of compliance to come into compliance and thus be eligible for federal aid.

Accordingly, Howe established an equal educational opportunity unit to work closely with the Office of the H.E.W. Secretary. He immediately began to cast about for appropriate leadership of it. The intent was that the two units together, one for enforcement and the other for support, would become an effective "one-two punch". In concert they would help resistant school districts overcome the gauntlet of the Civil Rights Act and take advantage of funds available under the Elementary and Secondary Education Act.

As the search for a director of this new unit got underway Howe recalled an incident that had occurred five years before when he was School Superintendent in Scarsdale, NY. He had been seeking candidates then for a vacant school principalship. A promising young fellow named Greg Anrig, principal of Battle Hill Junior High School in adjacent White Plains, had come to his attention as an interesting possibility for the job. So he invited him over for a talk. He told Anrig of the advantages of this career move including a hefty pay raise! The latter thanked him for the compliment of the interview and the potential raise. He then said he would stay right where he was regardless of compensation, because "the problems of American education are where I am not where you are" (Howe 1994). What he meant was that White Plains was a place with many more students from poor families and more people of color than Scarsdale, by a large margin.

In 1966, as Howe contemplated the potentially explosive situation the Johnson Administration faced, he recalled this brief exchange with the intense and polite yet reluctant young principal from White Plains. He concluded readily that he would be the right person to head the new technical assistance office at the U. S. Office of Education, the Division of Equal Educational Opportunity.

For his part Anrig had already changed jobs twice in those five years - from 1961 to 1966, first leaving White Plains to become school superintendent in a small district in western Massachusetts.   Whereas his talents and drive would undoubtedly have led in short order to the leadership of a larger district, he left Massachusetts in 1966 and joined the staff of the U.S. Office of Education as head of the Title III office, the so-called innovative programs unit.

It was at this juncture in the evolution of the federal role in education that Anrig's first major career shift brought him into the mainstream of significant national issues, in close contact with the work of Harold Howe and others on equal educational opportunity.   From this engagement he learned the powerful effect that a small group of dedicated people could have if they took effective action as an issue of great scope and complexity unfolded around them.

The work Anrig undertook in 1967 in the Division of Equal Educational Opportunity was complicated and full of dynamic tensions. The tasks stood right at the intersection of law enforcement on the one hand, i.e. suing for civil rights, and inducement on the other, i.e. providing on-site support for local efforts in civil rights. At the beginning of his tenure in this new post Anrig moved to subjugate the grant making role of the bureau to a new responsibility, providing direct technical assistance to local districts moving to desegregate their schools. He built an office of nearly twenty staff in Washington and added regional centers located in schools that could provide advice to local school and community leaders (McKettrick 1994).

Out in the field he dealt continuously and directly with judges, attorneys, school officials, teachers and parents; when the interchanges became intense - and they frequently did - he held to one simple line, "It's the law of the land!"   Interestingly, while this may have been a new line for him, it was hardly a new inclination. As Frank McKettrick, a former colleague of his, noted, the "dye" of his commitment to equal educational opportunity was not "cast" while he was at the Office of Education, rather "he came in that way" (Ibid).

"He was stubborn," said McKettrick of Anrig.   The challenges of the U.S.O.E. in the late '60's shaped and steeled that commitment. It added toughness rather than eroding it; he didn't become "burned out", he became "fired up". As it turned out he would need this level of enthusiasm - and more - when he assumed new challenges in the civil rights arena in subsequent assignments.

Desegregation Snapshots from Three Decades

The mid-sixties represented a watershed in the history of education policy setting in the United States. In a 1967 speech before the Forum of the Jewish Community Center in Cincinnati, the then U.S. Commissioner of Education Howe II surveyed the political and educational landscape as he saw it and assessed what was on the horizon for the education community.

> During the past three years no less than 38 major education bills have been enacted into law by the Congress -- it has been an exciting experience to participate in the launching of these programs. We have been part of what one observer described as the beginning of an educational revolution. (Howe 1967)

In that talk he also offered some perspectives that remind us that the same quandaries have dominated our discussions over the last several decades about how to improve education.

> We suppose that starting education earlier, bringing children who are three or four years old into the schools, may be part of the answer. We find some hope in trying to enlist the parents in the affairs of the school. We consider new and different systems of school organization and of teaching and of learning in an almost frantic search for the magic combination of new techniques and changed environmental influences which will somehow make successful in the schools a group of children with whom the schools are clearly all too unsuccessful now. (Ibid)

In the main, however, he used the occasion to issue a "call to arms" against segregation in the schools. He specifically challenged federal, state and local leaders to take up the charge against the blight that segregation represented. And he called the tide of new laws just passed "new leverage against old, ingrained problems: segregation not the least among them" (Ibid). Then later on in the same speech he provided this rationale:

> Too frequently and too easily we assume that building quality education into our segregated central city schools is a manageable task, but that planning for and developing integration is somehow unmanageable and therefore impossible. I know of no evidence which indicates that one approach is more viable than the other.
>
> We need to keep constantly before us a point which frequently gets lost in all the argument and counter argument about the academic advantages of integrated education. It is that the primary reason to get rid of segregated schools is not to bring about improvement in reading, writing and arithmetic. . . . The basic reason is the same as the reason for equality in voting rights, for equal access to public accommodations regardless of race, for employment opportunity without regard to race, religion, or national origin, and for open housing. . . . In allowing segregation to continue without continued efforts on all fronts - schools, housing and employment - to break it down, we endanger the future of our society, and we increase the possibility of reproducing South Africa in the United States without admitting it to ourselves. (Ibid)

With great foresight Howe then commented:

> What we adults have to accept is that children will sometimes be both the heroes and the victims of the changes which are underway. We need to do all we can to protect them, but from time to time we shall fail. (Ibid)

In wrapping up this landmark presentation he repeated the call:

> But the most important consideration is that the drive for equal educational opportunity has entered a critical phase. Today it is at last being waged in the only places and in the only way that can determine the ultimate outcome - in the states and local communities and at state and local initiative. (Ibid)

There are two things that are striking about this 1967 presentation. First is its optimism. While it reflects considerable sobriety about how difficult it will be to overcome the obstacles, its overall tone is extravagantly hopeful. Second is the sharp and clean delineation of the two main threads, improving schools on the one hand and giving every student a fair shake on the other. The threads relate; they are intertwined in several ways and at several points. But there is a point where they divide, and giving every student a fair shake stands alone on its own merits: the Constitutional guarantee of due process.

The years since Howe's call to arms have indeed been sobering, if not jolting, ones for the optimists. The prevailing attitude of most people today toward the salutary effects of desegregation is skepticism. For some, it is outright pessimism, and for a few, deep cynicism. One or a combination of these three has crept into our thinking and demonstrably affected our actions. Relatively few people in leadership positions today lead the charge Howe was attempting to mount, and even these individuals are more tempered, more restrained in the way they go about it.

What was the cause for this "downshift"? How much did it have to do with people's political leanings? How much is attributable to other factors? As part of the inquiry into this matter, let me offer a selective look at the many twists and turns of our collective thinking about the role of civil rights in education over the last three decades. While a crude sampling, the elements that I have chosen at least capture the progression that has taken place in the field since 1967.

In 1977, ten years after Howe's "call to arms", the U.S. Government commissioned a study on the role state leaders had played in school desegregation over the previous decade. The Stanford Research Institute conducted the study. It answers the question of what had happened to the "educational revolution" that Howe had heralded, a revolution in which state and local leaders would step forth to fulfill the mandate of school desegregation. Focusing in on the role of state education agencies, the report noted:

Of the 19 states visited or called, only 9 can be considered as having active desegregation programs in the same sense that they try to take positive or self-initiated steps at the SEA (State Education Agency) level to eliminate segregation at the LEA (local education agency or school district) level.

Of the nine states with active programs, however, only five have authority to identify schools with excessive or out-of-balance minority enrollments, to initiate desegregation actions, and to take enforcement steps to compel compliance. These five states -- Illinois, Massachusetts, New Jersey, New York and Pennsylvania -- are the only states considered to have a comprehensive state role; yet even these states are not free from problems, political pressures and citizen resistance . (The State Role in School Desegregation 1977)

Among the many implications of the study for future policy making, this topped the list.

Except for the handful of leaders already identified, states seem unlikely to voluntarily pursue desegregation on their own. Desegregation issues are politically sensitive and few political leaders at the state level appear willing to press them. (Ibid)

Massachusetts: A Picture Album
Bulging with Images

One of the States where leaders were willing to press for progress on desegregation was Massachusetts. When Anrig had become State Commissioner there in 1973 the educational rights of Black children in Boston were in contention. Loaded words and phrases like "desegregation", "racial isolation", "racial balance", "busing" infused a continuing public debate about elementary and secondary education in Boston in the late 60's and early 70's that had been vigorous throughout and at times vitriolic. Both the air and airwaves in Boston's neighborhoods were full of harangue on these topics.

In contrast to the arguments being made on the street or in the studio, those offered in court were much less muddled. Findings of fact and of law were indisputable. People in positions of power and responsibility had systematically denied Black children equal access to educational services in the City. Subsequent to the Federal Court decision in 1974 that attempted to right the situation, a booklet subtitled, "You Really Ought to Read This to Understand Boston's Shame" was published (Author's Recollection). It catalogued with great thoroughness the countless abuses of office and position by public officials in Boston ensuring that Black children did not receive equal access to education, thereby denying them due process of law.

Before the Federal Court action of 1974, the State Board of Education, under a 1960's State Law on Racial Balance, had borne the burden of protecting the rights of Black children in Boston. Of all the school desegregation cases across the country brought in the 60's under the Fourteenth Amendment to the U.S. Constitution - the due process clause - *only in Massachusetts was the state agency declared not liable as a defendant.* The Massachusetts State Board of Education was Anrig's employer.

Between 1974, when Garrity ruled, and 1981, when Anrig left the Commissioner's job for another post, the most intense battles over the desegregation of the Boston schools took place. Throughout this period there was a constant police presence in many of the schools, particularly the high schools. Persistent tension accompanied the buses that simultaneously unloaded Black youth at predominantly White South Boston High School and White youth at mainly Black Roxbury High School. Large numbers of White Bostonians reached out to their in-laws in towns south and west of Boston and enrolled their children in schools there rather than keep them in the turmoil-ridden city schools.

In the deliberations of public bodies during this period the rhetoric of resistance was constant and intense. Louise Day Hicks and her colleagues on the Boston School Committee, and later John Kerrigan and his on the same body, sought to undermine Garrity's Federal Court Order at every turn. The Judge for his part issued hundreds of subsidiary orders compelling everybody from the School Committee to the City Council, and from the chief administrators of the school system to the leaders of the teachers' union, to do their part in support of desegregation. The most hard-core neighborhood advocacy group, the South Boston Action Committee, organized public rally after public rally to engender open defiance of the Federal Court Order. Ray Flynn, then a State Representative, assisted the Committee (Author's Recollection). He later shed the association with the Action Committee and was elected Mayor of Boston.

More than once advocates from South Boston traveled in buses in the early morning hours to air their grievances on the front lawn of the State Education Commissioner's house in Needham, a suburb west of Boston (Author's Recollection). At Freedom House in Roxbury over those early years, Black leaders met at times on a round-the-clock basis to plot public and behind-the-scenes strategies in support of the Judge's Order (Jackson 1994). These were the main contextual elements that formed both foreground and background to the work Anrig did to attend to Civil Rights during his tenure in Massachusetts.

From the beginning of his term as Commissioner he knew he was "on the spot" in terms of upholding his own personal oath to the U.S. Constitution. In his first fifteen months on the job, the time prior to the Garrity ruling, he quickly assumed the role of standard bearer for the position the State Board of Education had maintained under State law since the 60's. When the Federal Court Order came down, he aligned himself squarely with the Judge, directing the full force of his office and the resources of the Department to the plethora of difficulties that arose in the wake of the Order.

He took this tack in the face of a steady stream of strong and at times violent pressures from local community groups. He did this despite an outpouring of negative commentary from nearly all sectors and levels of government - legislative and executive, city, state and federal. He did this despite a "media blitz" that often left one wondering whether it was Boston or Belfast that was the point of origin of the story. He did this in the face of threats of violence to his family and his own person. He did this because he believed deeply that there was no clearer mandate for a person than a rule of law that warranted fair remedy for a justifiably aggrieved party.

After eight arduous years of working <u>with</u> the Federal Court but <u>against</u> the grain of popular sentiment to attend to civil rights, the outgoing State Education Commissioner wrote Judge Garrity. The letter was dated July, 1981. He outlined for the Court the path the parties would need to follow to allow the Federal Court to disengage FINALLY from the affairs of the Boston Public Schools. The letter focused on the issues of standards by which to judge compliance, responsibility for implementation, a system for internal monitoring of the longstanding Court Order, and the future access of the parties to the Court to resolve disputes. It also detailed twelve areas which the Court might incorporate as standing orders into a final decree (Anrig 1981). Judge Garrity, as he had throughout the long struggle, used the contents of the letter as the basis for subsequent actions he took on the case (Garrity 1994).

Nonetheless, thirteen years later, in 1994, when I was doing the research for this book, the Morgan Case had still not been concluded. In that elapsed time the shortfalls of the school system had hardly been eliminated. A parade of school administrators had passed through the school superintendent's chair, some barely grazing its felt cushion before they were on to assignments elsewhere. The public deliberations of the School Committee remained more like a circus routine than a meeting of people entrusted with the educational welfare of thousands of children. The enrollment of the city schools continued to shrink. By all accounts, i.e. the countless commissioned studies and reports of Blue Ribbon panels, there were some educational bright spots. Yet it was still hit or miss as to whether one's child would receive a decent education in the Boston Public Schools.

When interviewed in his chambers in September, 1994, Judge Garrity offered up what he referred to as the second to final order in the Morgan Case. It was an order that emphasized, among other things, the integration of the teaching and administrative staff of the Boston Public Schools. This had been an intractable matter continually pushed aside by more pressing matters in the years preceding. With a slight smile, the Judge, now partially retired, suggested that the case might indeed be closed before the year ended, some twenty-two after it had first been brought (Garrity 1994).

Impressions the Album Leaves

The collective path we have followed over the past twenty seven years has been circuitous, torturous. In 1967 Harold Howe sought to engage the energies of state and local leaders to address and overcome the challenges posed by the conjunction of great forces: the warrants of school improvement framed against the mandate of school desegregation. Except in a very few places the energies did not engage. Local and state leaders for the most part remained on the sidelines while Federal Judges issued compelling rulings and sought to effect compliance within enormously complex sets of circumstances within state and local jurisdictions.

On the most dramatic fronts - the streets of Charlotte-Mecklenburg, North Carolina; Birmingham, Alabama; Roxbury and South Boston, Massachusetts; and countless other places large and small - there was over these years great tumult, vociferous and vitriolic rhetoric, and much spilled blood. On less dramatic fronts there was increasing weariness and consequent inaction in the face of disparate points of view and pervasive fear. Overall there was a blunting of the edge on the blade that Howe so clearly brandished almost three decades before. In practical terms there really was no way that the banner the Federal Courts had carried could be upheld in the absence of sustained support from local and state leaders.

Even a cursory review of the progression of events from 1967 to 1994 shows how government, including the courts, has become much more tentative in its moves to guarantee equal access for all to adequate schooling. For those who have suffered persistent disenfranchisement, the present disposition is exceedingly bad news. The only good news - perhaps - is that flows of events like the one just cited have encouraged us to be more sober and circumspect. Certainly they have pushed us to be considerably more philosophical, to take more of the long view about serious social change. The best we can say is that this may yield more durable positive change in the long run.

It is signally important for our purpose here to have identified some of the channel markers we have passed as a society since 1967. We can thereby better understand the backdrop against which Anrig began to interact with the issues of civil rights and school improvement on the national stage. We are also able to see how his initial interactions with the issues shaped his thinking and actions throughout a career dedicated to equal access for all.

Expanding Civil Rights beyond Race

The most acute angle on desegregation and integration issues in this nation is that of racial identity. The work that consumed Anrig while he was in Washington and in Massachusetts was related to racial integration in the public schools. His experience in the Bay State offered him as well the unique opportunity to exert leadership in securing equal education opportunity for groups other than African Americans.

In the Commonwealth, in the late 60's and early 70's, there had been a series of laws passed that guaranteed the educational rights of a variety of recognizable groups, including Non-English speaking students, females and students with physical and mental disabilities. Anrig eagerly assumed full responsibility for the implementation of these laws. He used his considerable organizational skills and acumen about bureaucratic functioning to develop and disseminate regulations in support of the laws. He applied the full force of his statutory role to see that all who were due services received them. He set up appropriate mechanisms to hear appeals from those who felt they were denied services. All of this effort was directed at making the laws more of a reality in the lives of people who worked in and attended schools. In the chapter that follows there is a more substantial discussion of the actions he took and the effects they had.

But for Busing Nearly New York State Commissioner

By 1977 Anrig's work in Massachusetts on equal educational opportunity was in full swing. The desegregation of the Boston Schools had by this time become a full-blown Promethean struggle between the Federal Court, assisted by the State Board of Education, and the Boston School Committee, bent on expressing both overt and covert resistance to the despised Court order. The Massachusetts precedent of guaranteeing the rights of handicapped children to an appropriate education had been written into Federal Law, in the form of the Education of All Handicapped Children Act. The State Board of Education in Massachusetts was pushing forward on the implementation of the Transitional Bilingual Education Act passed six years earlier. The Board had as well just issued new rules for the implementation of Chapter 622, the state's law on gender equity in education.

In the midst of this flow of intense activity on equal education opportunity, a possible career move caught Anrig's eye. There were perhaps few posts in the country he was more interested in than that of New York State Commissioner of Education. It was the state education post that had the most revered traditions and the greatest span of authority and responsibility. It was also the post that James Allen had held before he went to Washington as U.S. Commissioner of Education in 1970. Anrig had deep respect for Allen, particularly because of his concern for teaching and learning in the schools and his demonstrated commitment to equal educational opportunity.

At times he evidenced this regard for Allen in ways that some might consider old fashioned. Even after Anrig had worked as Allen's closest aide in Washington for nearly two years, he still referred to him as "Dr. Allen". In contrast, those with whom he would converse, most of whom barely knew the man, referred to him as "Jim" (Author's Recollection). Allen's untimely death in a plane crash soon after leaving his post in Washington undoubtedly intensified Anrig's esteem for him and the posts he had held.

So when the job came open Anrig entered his name for consideration. Readily he emerged as a strong contender. Although it is difficult to reassemble all the pieces of the end game on the search, the job might well have been his (Author's Recollection). There was but one sticking point between him and the New York State Board of Regents. And it was major, his position on school desegregation. This he knew because of the disagreements that had in part led the Board of Regents to dismiss Joe Nyquist, the last person to hold the job. Even though he was aware of this looming ambivalence Anrig pursued his candidacy. Perhaps he thought he could convince the Board of the rightness of his position on civil rights, a position that was integral to the legacy of James Allen.

In a move that in all likelihood scotched his chances for the job, Anrig explained his position on desegregation in a letter to the Regents at the final hour of the search. Here are key excerpts:

1. As a matter of legal policy, where there have been official actions or inactions, the effects of which are to segregate children by race in public schools, you have a de jure situation for which the U.S. Supreme Court has set standards for a constitutional remedy. . . . 2. As a matter of educational policy, I believe public school officials have an affirmative responsibility to eliminate or reduce the racial identifiability of schools regardless of cause. . . . 3. The use of techniques other than transportation should be utilized fully as is recommended in your [The Regent's] 1968 Statement. My experience with many northern and southern school districts, however, continues to prove that voluntary means alone are insufficient to eliminate or significantly reduce the racial identifiability of schools especially in larger districts. . . . 4. The location of pupil residence and of school buildings is fixed. Where this results in racial identifiability of schools, transportation is inevitable if desegregation is to be achieved after techniques other than transportation have been tried. (Anrig 1977)

The last sentence quoted above undoubtedly sealed the outcome: busing had become a significant political liability by that time in most parts of the country. Anrig stayed on for four more years as Massachusetts Commissioner.

At ETS Civil Rights Currents Remain Strong

When Anrig left Massachusetts in 1981 and arrived in Princeton to confront the numerous issues that dogged educational testers, it would have been easy for him to push the civil right issues into the background. Certainly there was plenty to deal with at ETS without confronting the knotty problems of equality of educational opportunity for dispossessed groups. The credibility of the testing industry was on the line. ETS, the largest testing firm, had been singled out as the grand culprit because of its size, its "presumed wealth and secrecy", and its phlegmatic resistance to moves by legislative bodies to effect greater disclosure of test questions. A subsequent chapter, "Reestablishing the Educational Testing Service", contains considerably more on the ameliorative role Anrig played in this context.

Despite the daunting challenges the ETS job brought, he maintained, even strengthened, his commitment to civil rights. He broadened an already expansive portfolio on equal educational opportunity by adding in other complementary elements. A good example was the strategic alliances he built with the National Association for the Advancement of Colored People (NAACP) and the Urban League to assure greater fairness in the testing of minority children and youth (Horne 1994).

He also established strong bonds with the Historically Black Colleges and Universities (HBCU). The set of agreements he negotiated personally with HBCU leaders supported aims similar to those of the NAACP and Urban League agreements. In addition, they offered special opportunities for HBCU staff and students to engage in research on testing issues (Albright 1994).

Finally he intervened personally to prevent several jurisdictions - Arkansas and Texas, for example - from using the results of the National Teachers Exam in ways that would harm minority teachers. The NTE, he argued, was designed to screen teacher candidates upon university graduation, not to winnow out incompetent teachers once on the job.

The View from Downstream

It has been over forty years since the U.S. Supreme Court ruled in favor of the plaintiffs in the case of Brown vs. the Topeka, Kansas Board of Education. The essence of that decision was that segregated schooling of Black children was inherently inferior education and that it had to be eliminated "root and branch." The Brown decision provoked a flood of activity in school desegregation in this country, the spillover of which has not yet been stemmed. Witness the continuing struggle of the Federal Judiciary with the issue.

As I write these pages, the U.S. Supreme Court is about to rule on another "Kansas case", that of Kansas City, Missouri. The "lines" in this case are markedly more obscure than those of its predecessor. Money and administrative responsibility are far removed from the more fundamental question of whether separate schooling is inherently unequal.

At the headwaters of these actions on civil rights was the turbulence in the South in the 1960's. It was indeed a boiling, tangled stretch of water for us as a nation as almost any piece of reclaimed news footage from the time will attest. By the same token the conflict produced some extraordinarily positive changes in the social make-up and economic capacity of the region in which it all started. Certainly desegregation was as responsible as any factor for the economic, social and cultural renaissance that is taking place in the South. Those years, when the South felt the brunt, were also the last in which there was aggressive leadership from a U.S. President and Congress on the issues of racial integration.

By the early 70's the appetite of the majority of the voting electorate for activism on school desegregation was diminished. This shift was clearly reflected in the policies and actions of the country's elected officials. In 1977, for example, Anrig penned a note to Chester Finn, who was working in the White House at the time Anrig was serving as James Allen's Executive Assistant in the Office of Education. Finn was writing a book on the Nixon years, and Anrig was responding to draft text. His response serves as a summative reflection on the Nixon Administration's contribution to desegregation efforts.

> I found no 'lessening of tension', much outright duplicity and no constitutional action during this period except when absolutely forced to act by the order of the federal judiciary. The progress by 1970 that you refer to was despite the Executive and would have to be credited to decisions within the judiciary to start issuing orders covering large groups of school districts, rather than going one district at a time. Ironically the 'Nixon contribution' during this time was to precipitate great leaps in the case law of desegregation, mostly as a result of Administration inaction and recalcitrance in federal courts. (Anrig 1977)

There were a number of reasons for the declining constituency support for school desegregation. One was that the task was messy and difficult to accomplish. There was just too much negative fallout in mainstream communities. Furthermore, the apparent successes experienced in one region of the country, the South, were, it turned out, not readily transportable to other regions of the country, most particularly the more populous and influential North.

One of the lead stories of Northern desegregation for almost a decade was the Boston Schools Crisis. A large majority of the voting public surely did not perceive what was happening there in the mid-70's as a successful venture in school integration. That the turn of events in this city was in large part due to the outright resistance of local leaders to the rule of law is really not consequential. The upshot in terms of public perception was that integration was a lot more attractive in theory than it was in practice. If at all attractive in practice it was because it could conveniently be foisted on someone else's community, not mine. Specifically, as the sixties turned into the seventies, the "right" place had been the rural conservative South, not the more "liberal" urban North.

Since Lyndon Johnson no U.S. President has actively supported desegregation efforts. Two of the seven Presidents since Johnson - the two Democrats, Carter and Clinton - have made passing gestures at its significance in the form of speeches and ceremonies (Orfield 1994). None has taken definitive action on behalf of the large body of case law supporting the civil rights of minority groups, particularly African Americans. This is not hard to understand. Like "Gays in the military" it is one of those extraordinarily controversial issues in which the engagement of politicians provides them with more potential to lose votes than to gain them.

As executive and legislative action on civil rights at both federal and state levels lessened, civil rights activists, rather than giving up their portfolio, broadened it. The portfolio came to include ethnic groups other than African Americans, i.e. women and girls and physically and mentally disabled people. Equally if not more important, the bedrock of civil rights, due process for all, found its way into almost every aspect of our lives. It began to pervade our thought processes on how people were hired and fired from jobs, how they gained acceptance to one college or another, and whether they could dress in certain ways for public tasks like attending school or being on the job.

Anrig remained a zealot for civil rights throughout his professional career. The evolving currents of the nation's concern for civil rights over the past three decades depict to a significant extent his own evolution. His intensity on the issue, his passion to make it right for persons disadvantaged in the eyes of others, stayed constant throughout and distinguished him from the majority of the electorate.

Like his fellow citizens, the river of his concern for civil rights broadened and deepened. The number of constituencies and settings where the concern appeared proliferated for him as they did for the majority of the populace. Paralleling them, he turned his attention to the rights of people other than Black Americans. Paralleling them, he began to apply his energy to the requisites of due process in multiple arenas. His focus in the last decade, for example, was fairness in testing, the multiple and complex processes used in society to sort people with regard to innate and acquired capacities.

Unlike most of his peers, Anrig remained a warrior, full of passion and will when it came to matters of equal opportunity. It is patently clear why this was so: he had a life long commitment to democratic ideals as manifested in integrated communities. He expressed this commitment when he was growing up in New Jersey, affirmed it when he first became an educator, and expanded its scope when he went to Washington in the heady 60's, to Boston in the testy 70's, and finally back to New Jersey in the somewhat prosaic 80's.

It is highly unlikely that we will move forward as a democratic nation until we have confronted head on one of our most serious social diseases, racism. Like the pollution of the globe, racism divides us from ourselves and thereby has the potential to destroy us, specifically by taking away our capacity to live in requisite harmony with each other. Eliminating this negative presence means we will collectively be able to attend in earnest to the civil rights of all our citizens. Consequently we will unlock the potential for good that exists in the communities that make up this nation.

To eliminate the negative and make room for the positive will require the honest and active engagement of our leaders with the tough challenges of implementing Constitutional commitments. Whether Anrig was right or wrong in his approach to civil rights - I believe he was right - is less important in the larger scheme of things than that he was fully and forthrightly engaged with the issue. He did not dodge it. He was one with it to begin with, and he continued to make himself one with it throughout his life. He openly brought it into the public forum and sought its resolution. We need to do this ourselves. And we desperately need leaders in the public arena who will do the same. The stakes are big, our own collective welfare and that of the generations that follow.

Chapter 5

MASSACHUSETTS SERVICE

In 1971 Martha Zeigler moved her family from a Long Island to a Boston suburb. One of her children was a seven year old girl who was autistic. When they lived on Long Island it never occurred to Martha to approach the local public school system to seek educational services for her daughter. There was just no solid legal or financial reason for the schools there to provide the special assistance that would have been necessary. Within five years of her move to Massachusetts, the public schools were serving the educational needs of her daughter on a consistent basis.
From my interview with Martha Zeigler

"Anrig adjusted Massachusetts education policy to the needs of the modern world." - A comment Harold Howe made during our interview

The Decision to Undertake State Service

Anrig's stint in Washington was the first but not the only time his career veered from the traditional path. It happened again in 1973 when he turned to state service, becoming

Commissioner of Education for the Commonwealth of Massachusetts. He described the background of this decision in a speech he made in 1980 on "Local Control and State Responsibility -- Keeping the Tensions Creative":

> When I was at the University of Massachusetts in the early 70's, one of my staff asked for some career counseling. After trying to be helpful to him, he asked what my career goals were. I replied that at that point in my life there were only five jobs in the United States that I was interested in, and they were all state education commissioner positions.
>
> My decision to become a commissioner was a very conscious choice. After being a local and federal administrator, I was convinced that the "action" in education increasingly was going to be at the state level. I reached that conclusion because I felt that educational authority at the local level was becoming fragmented, buffeted and beleaguered. At the Federal level the effects of Vietnam and Watergate were quickly eroding what once appeared to be a national commitment to education. This vacuum, it seemed to me, provided a real opportunity and need for leadership at the state level. (Anrig 1980)

The Context Circa 1973

When Anrig arrived on the Massachusetts State scene, the air was full of tension and anticipation. For nearly nine years the State Board of Education had been embroiled in a standoff with the Boston School Committee over the matter of racial balance in the City's Schools. The Board, although less visibly, had also been attempting to implement other equally demanding pieces of education legislation that afforded new rights to special groups.

The state legislature, formally known as the Great and General Court of the Commonwealth, had passed a Racial Balance Act in the mid-sixties, a gender equity provision in the late sixties, a Transitional Bilingual Education Act in 1971, and landmark Special Education Legislation in 1972. The first of these warranted the integration of the Commonwealth's city school systems, most particularly Boston, but also Springfield,

Cambridge, New Bedford and Fall River. The second mandated that female students had the same rights to educational services as male students. The third specified the entitlement of students whose first language was not English to appropriate educational services in two languages. The fourth said that the public schools had to seek out and serve physically and mentally disabled youngsters, age 3 to 21, in the least restrictive setting possible. This meant that large numbers of handicapped students would be joining their peers in public school classrooms.

The Desegregation Crisis in Microcosm

In the last chapter I described the flow of events relating to the desegregation of the Boston Public Schools. From the broadbrush coverage provided, the reader may not have been able to get a genuine feel for the actual human interactions that made up those events. These interactions were intense, sometimes explosively so, because they quickly brought basic values to the surface and provided a ready forum for them to clash. This was particularly true for Anrig and those with whom he worked at the center of the fray.

One person who had been intimately involved almost from the beginning of the dispute was Rae Cecilia Kipp. A cherubic woman, barely five feet tall, perpetually adorned with a disarming smile and a tightly managed hairdo, Kipp was in 1973 the chair of the State Board of Education. She was a staunch advocate of education and a fierce proponent of equal rights. Her support of Anrig to become the Board's chief staff person was undoubtedly related to his performance on desegregation issues while in Washington in the years before.

The Board she headed in the mid-seventies was caught in a tight vice. On the one hand it was attempting to fulfill a state legislative mandate for school integration; on the other, it was being publicly pummeled by almost every elected official in Boston, both state and local, for trying to do so. A seeming contradiction, until one recalls that desegregation was a cause acceptable to many in theory, but best implemented in someone else's backyard in practice.

Rae Kipp had felt the heat of her difficult assignment first hand. About the time Anrig was coming on as Commissioner, the State's Attorney General, Robert Quinn, sought a face-to-face meeting with the State Board of Education on the matter of the Board's active stance on school desegregation in Boston. The gist of his request was that the Board back off a bit in response to the mounting opposition from several powerful people. In contrast to Kipp, Quinn was a large person, over six feet and heavy set. After he made his overture to the Board, Rae Kipp moved from behind the table where the Board sat, approached the Attorney General, looked straight up at him from her five foot frame and said in no uncertain terms,"NO" (Daly 1994)!

It is important to remember that the pecking order between the State Board of Education and the State Attorney General was hardly ambiguous. The AG was one of the top four elected officials in the Commonwealth and its chief law enforcement officer. The Board was a creature of the Executive branch of State Government, composed of nine solid, but politically weak citizens appointed by the Governor for terms longer than his own. It had no direct access to the public purse. For financial resources the Board had to plead with the Governor and ultimately convince the Legislature. Its main functions were to carry out state education law as established by the Legislature, to appoint an executive officer, a Commissioner, and to oversee the operations of the Department of Education, the thousand-person organization the Commissioner headed.

So, in a very real sense the Board had less leverage than the Attorney General on just about every issue. On school desegregation, however, it had two things he did not: moral high ground and a lot less political baggage. Since its members were appointed rather than elected, they had few debts to pay, few obligations to fulfill. In a Taoist sense the Board's very lack of power in the circumstances as described gave it all that it needed. Its source was the freedom to act their conscience in a less unencumbered, more pure manner. It may be that this sort of power is exactly what we need more of in our social dealings, particularly on matters like race relations where denial and rejection are likely to set in after initial attempts at resolution.

Denial and rejection, compounded with fear and ignorance, were in the main what fueled the tensions around racial integration of the Boston Schools. In the decades preceding the seventies the negative energy inherent in these factors had steadily accumulated as disenfranchised immigrants and indigenous peoples of different colors and ethnic backgrounds were layered one upon another in close quarters within the boundaries of the City. And people of lighter color, more distant ethnic roots and greater wealth left behind the growing tensions and antipathies of the city for a better life in the suburbs.

There was in addition a defining reality of public affairs in Massachusetts that made the situation even more awkward. While the State was supposed to be the superordinate entity over the City, the fact of the matter was that most of the money and political power base within the State lay within the City of Boston. A similar situation exists in almost all states where the capital is the largest city and accounts for a large proportion of the population of the state.

It was extraordinarily difficult for the Board and Commissioner to maintain any foothold at all, with such strong forces vying for power in the middle of a titanic struggle over basic values. Commenting on just exactly how difficult it was, Sandra Lynch, Anrig's General Counsel, told the following story. When Michael Dukakis was elected Governor in November, 1974, his General Counsel wrote the State Board of Education and the Commissioner seeking a private meeting with them to discuss the desegregation crisis. The Governor's intent, it appeared, was to see if the Board might adopt a more moderate position than the staunch one it had been holding, a position recently reinforced by Judge Garrity's June, 1974 ruling.

There sat the Board and Anrig with a new Governor in the first months of his term, a person with whom it was essential to develop an effective working relationship. Anrig well understood that the viability of the Board as an institution was under threat, and his own job too might well be on the line. With Lynch's help, he deliberated the alternatives and decided to recede politely from the request of the Governor's Office for a private meeting, citing the recently passed Open Meeting Law (Lynch 1994). That measure, sometimes called the "Sunshine Law", required all public bodies to announce their meetings ahead of time and make them as accessible to the public as possible.

This was a most adept move under the circumstances. No formal "transaction " between the Governor's Office and the State Board occurred on the matter of school desegregation at that point. The Governor's staff was apparently reluctant to have such a conversation "in the sunshine." The State Board's position stayed firm behind that of the Federal Judge. Anrig, and the Board, had quietly prevailed in the face of a push by a powerful force, at least for the moment. Furthermore, the story did not reach the <u>Boston Globe</u>, as vigilant as it was on the most minute aspects of the desegregation saga. The only visible effect of the whole episode was heavy perspiration over deeply furrowed brows in the Office of the Education Commissioner.

Living the desegregation crisis day to day required intestinal fortitude on the part of all concerned. There was the overpowering fear of the parents, both Black and White, for the welfare of their children. That fear mounted each morning as the children were transported by bus from the relative safety of their home communities to the "foreign territory" of South Boston or Roxbury. There was the tension and apprehension of the children as they passed through portals where many of the adults, both in the neighborhood and the building, did not want them there. In a late sixties speech quoted earlier, Harold Howe had said that "we as adults have to accept that children will sometimes be both heroes and victims of the changes that are underway." This was indeed what was happening in Boston less than a decade later.

Heroism and victimization were present too in the lives of the relatively small number of public officials who oversaw the decisions to integrate the Boston City Schools. Not too many days passed at the State Department of Education without a threatening phone call from the South Boston resistance movement or an anonymous letter suggesting the possibility of physical harm (Author's Recollection). Judge Garrity himself, upon rendering a decision in the desegregation case, was for several years after attended by Federal Marshalls, both at work and at home (Garrity 1994). Even as minor an actor as I was at the time - the head of planning in the State Department of Education - I too received the occasional threatening phone call or letter.

In the previous chapter I recounted the visitation by several hundred anti-integration advocates to the Anrig home in Needham. These had to be deeply threatening events for him and his family, since they put at risk the base of support he most deeply cherished and was most quick to defend. There were, in addition, other less overt attacks that must have left him wondering exactly what he had got himself into in Massachusetts. Walking down Bolyston Street one day in Boston with Michael Daly, his chief deputy, the two of them crossed paths with one of Boston's City Councillors. Without hesitation, the Councillor blurted, "Michael, I like you, but I don't like the company you keep." After an intervening second or two, Anrig turned to Daly and asked if it might aid the latter's reputation if he walked on the other side of the street (Daly 1994).

Reflections on the Crisis

Regardless of circumstances and outcomes - the too high price that some thought then, and many think now, was paid for Boston school desegregation - Anrig believed that the cost of not heeding the U.S. Constitution would be even higher in the long run. This would be true even if that long run extended beyond his lifetime.

Right now, the jury is still out on the effects of desegregation on the Boston community and its schools. Clearly there has been substantial White flight; but this is true of other cities too, even those that did not suffer major desegregation crises. The leadership of the schools remains a mixed lot, both the lay governors, i.e. the School Committee, and the administrators; although there is presently some hope engendered because the Committee is now appointed by the Mayor rather than elected by the populace. In fact, the

Committee recently hired a Superintendent of noted stature as an educator and skill as an administrator.

The quality of education, despite Herculean efforts by many, still remains more mediocre than good. The ill effects of racism, while constrained, are as debilitating now as they were two decades ago. A recent incident like the Carol Stewart murder readily opens deep wounds that exist below a thin veneer of social peace, causing everyone to question whether race relations can ever improve in Boston. (Both Carol Stewart and her husband, who murdered her, were White. In the aftermath he sought to deflect his guilt onto a fictional Black assailant.)

In the mid-seventies Anrig came to Massachusetts confident and optimistic. He wagered that the line, "It's the law of the land." would carry the same weight as it had in Southern school districts with which he had worked in the sixties. And he maintained that the better side of people would ultimately prevail in the interests of integrated education. The challenge turned out to be more complex and nettlesome in a Northern clime than it had been in a Southern one. As things turned from bad to worse in Boston, Anrig himself became fond of repeating a comment that one of his Southern colleagues had made in a speech about school integration. "We welcome you Northern saints to the company of us Southern sinners" (Author's Recollection).

Gary Orfield, one of the nation's leading experts on school integration, suggested that two factors had to be present for the Boston situation to come out better than it did. First, there had to be resolute commitment and positive action by respected community leaders behind the moves to desegregate the schools. Second, surrounding suburban communities had to be more significantly engaged in crafting a solution, that is, in the actual placement of students to achieve racially balanced classrooms. Boston, with less than three quarters of a million people in a metropolitan area of over three million, was too small to do it by itself. Neither of these factors was present (Orfield 1994).

A Promise Kept, To Educate Handicapped Pupils

As if desegregation was not enough, Anrig's advent as Commissioner coincided with the passage of a new law in Massachusetts. Chapter 766, as it was called, guaranteed the educational rights of handicapped children. It would readily, even before it was fully implemented in Massachusetts, become the model for the 1976 Federal Law, the so-called Education of All Handicapped Children Act. Both the forerunner and the Federal law that superseded it mandated complex procedures to ensure that handicapped children and their parents received their due from the public schools. That due was an appropriate education in the least restrictive environment.

While the Massachusetts Legislature had passed Chapter 766 and the Governor had signed it, the "lion's share" of the work was still undone when Anrig came into office. In 1973 the entitlements the law contained were already provoking considerable resistance from significant elements of the educational community, particularly local school boards. They felt that the law placed too many burdens on them. Pervasive cynicism on the part of leaders at all levels reinforced this widening resistance. Since much of the state legislation of the 60's had gone unimplemented, why not assume the same fate for Chapter 766?

Anrig, to the contrary and fully in character, took the new law very seriously. He never doubted that the State Board of Education and the Department could fulfill its intent, and thereby relieve the plight of children who desperately needed but had not been provided appropriate educational services. That the implementation of this complex social measure - today we take it as a given - proceeded as far and as quickly as it did is directly attributable in significant part to his insistence and skill.

Martha Zeigler, who had come to Massachusetts from New York in search of an appropriate education for her autistic daughter, found it a real possibility in her newly adopted state. In fairly short order she also became the head of the principal organization in the Commonwealth that sought an appropriate education for all children regardless of disability. In her view the stipulations of the law became a reality in great part because of Anrig's efforts. She said, "He had so much moral energy that it carried over to teachers and principals, who then wanted to do the right thing" (Zeigler 1994).

In actuality there were many fronts on which Anrig worked, dispensing his moral energy on behalf of educating handicapped children. Over the crucial early years of his administration, from 1973-77, he jawboned and prodded, even embarrassed local school district leadership into doing what the law called for. He convinced a progressively less progressive State Legislature not to back down from its original commitment to the law. He wrestled an increasingly skeptical Governor's Office into maintaining pace on implementation in spite of mounting criticism from municipal officials. He went to court against flagrant violators of the Law. Incessantly he pushed all agencies of State Government to guarantee the rights of institutionalized children to an appropriate education.

He also channeled federal discretionary funds to needed capacities that would support the law, such as an office for the fair hearing of individual appeals. And finally he conferred, endlessly it seemed, with state mental and public health officials to determine which agencies would be responsible for which supportive services; for these were the keys to an appropriate education for certain handicapped children. Martha Zeigler recalls one instance in which Anrig, off to the side, asked her to plead with Federal officials to find Massachusetts out of compliance on a key financial provision of the Education For All Handicapped Children Act. Were this the case the State would be eligible for greater assistance than it would have been if it were in compliance (Zeigler 1994).

His efforts were not only dogged, they were effective. Districts and schools identified many more handicapped children in the 70's and designed and implemented new programs of study for them. An increasing number of these programs were carried out in regular classrooms, with handicapped children learning alongside fellow students. For the first time in American history it seemed possible that schools could help remove, rather than reinforce, the stigmas applied to handicapped pupils. Such terms as "retarded" and "crippled" were at last becoming outmoded.

Regardless of one's views about the rightness of the public policy that Chapter 766 espoused or the wisdom of the increased allocation of public resources it entailed, the thoroughness with which it was implemented is impressive. Clearly no government official could have accomplished this without the persistent and powerful support of outside advocates, of which there were plenty like Martha Zeigler. What is equally true is that no set of advocates could have achieved such penetrating impact on the educational infrastructure without the ardent complicity of able officials. As Sandra Lynch, Anrig's general counsel, said, "When the special needs law was handed to him, it had no reality - he made it real" (Lynch 1994).

Schooling's Infrastructure, Finance

The most subtle but potent flow of energy in any field within the public domain is the distribution of resources, principally money. How much money is available to get something done? How and among whom is it distributed? And what actions are deemed legitimate with whatever dollars are made available? These are the core questions of educational finance.

In 1973 Massachusetts school finance was governed by a state law called Chapter 70. It provided for state reimbursement of eligible local expenses on a formula that was intended to give disproportionate aid to property-poor school districts. As is the case with all school aid formulas after they have been in place for several years, Chapter 70 was, by the mid-seventies, showing its flaws. And these flaws were even more pronounced than they ordinarily would have been, because the State Legislature had been increasingly unwilling to fund the formula at 100% of legally recognized need.

The law, for example, did not include the aid necessary for districts to conduct special education or vocational education programs. These were provided for under separate formulas not tied to districts' property wealth.   Nor were local property assessments built into the formula based on fair market values, so there was wide variance between districts in how property wealth was in fact being calculated.   Adding insult to injury, perennial underfunding was detracting even more from the law's power to aid poor localities.   At the 1973 funding level of 65% reimbursement of eligible expenses, the law was a pretty weak equalizing measure.

The aims that Anrig had in mind for state aid reform were few and simple.   He wanted to increase the state share of expenses for public schooling and to have the formula for school aid funded as close to 100% of local needs as possible.   He also sought to incorporate different program needs into the expense side of the formula, i.e. to fold in as many of the special programs like vocational education as possible into one needs-based formula.

His strategy for achieving these ends was equally simple. At the top of the list was building the capacity of the Department to analyze the workings of the current formula and the implications of potential changes to it.   The Legislature was at the center of the political battles over the distribution of resources, not the Board and the Commissioner.   Therefore the best the latter could do was to become authoritative in the eyes of those at the center of those battles.   In becoming a useful, even an essential analytic resource, Anrig believed that he and the Board could become a player at the table and eventually have their positions heard and possibly even adopted.   Specifically, what he did was to establish a small planning and research office in the Department that reported directly to him.   He staffed it with able policy analysts and ensured that it had access to data systems that could generate renderings of the present formula's effects as well as simulations of proposed alternatives.

Armed with these analyses, Anrig then positioned himself as a perennial keynote speaker at the annual state conference on state aid to education, attended by some of the most influential leaders in the State.   And lastly, he established and led a working coalition of all the major interest groups in education, the associations that represented teachers, administrators, school board members and others.   The sole purpose of the coalition was to formulate and advocate a common position on state aid reform.

These staging tactics, combined with dogged perseverance, finally paid off in 1978. The Legislature passed a monumental state aid revision, called the Boverini-Collins Bill, named after the Chairmen of the Education Committees in the House and Senate. It may as well have carried Anrig's name, since it fulfilled almost all the aims he had set for the revision of the State's approach to providing aid to school districts.

With classic irony, much of the work Anrig and others did on state aid unraveled within three years of the passage of Boverini-Collins. With the enactment of Proposition 2 1/2, the Commonwealth effectively rolled back its prior commitments to state support of local district efforts. It did this by putting a cap of 2 and 1/2% on all local property tax assessments calculated at fair market value. This prevented localities from spending at the levels they may have wanted to on their principal area of responsibility, schooling. And in turn it reduced overall state support, since state aid was tied to the level of local expenditure.

Anrig's legacy in state aid reform may lie as much in the areas of effective political advocacy and deft public affairs administration as they do in the efficacy of the particular measure with which he is associated, Boverini-Collins. He wisely established a new capacity in the Department that made the Board and himself credible partners in high-level deliberations on state aid, decision-making arenas that normally excluded members of his organization. In complementary fashion, he solidified a critical mass of political support for change on state aid within the broader educational community of the state. When he needed them, at crucial points in legislative deliberations, both the voices of his allies and the relevance of his data were brought into play, to significant effect.

People Management

One of the most complicated arenas of public affairs leadership is decision making about the lives of other people.

Recruiting, hiring, supervising, promoting, demoting and firing other people take as much time and psychological energy as any function a public affairs leader performs. It also presents as many ethical dilemmas and results in as much debilitating litigation, if not more, than other functions.

In many respects Anrig was a master of people management. When he was good, he was excellent; and there is much to learn from how he handled key situations. At the same time he was not without his Achilles' heels. Both aspects are revealed in the stories that follow.

Joe Robinson had been General Counsel in the Department of Education, forever it seemed, when Anrig arrived to take over as Commissioner. Robinson's main function had been to respond to legal matters that turned up on the desks of local school administrators or the tables of local school boards. As an on-call advisor he was accomplished and therefore well respected throughout the Commonwealth. Within a short time after his arrival, the exigencies of the Boston crisis and the multiple challenges of implementing new state laws left little doubt in Anrig's mind that a new orientation and set of skills were required in the Office of the General Counsel.

He moved quickly in 1974 to secure the services of a young Assistant Attorney General fresh out of law school to assist with the new challenges the Department was facing. An obvious dilemma: what to do about the incumbent counsel who, beside his credibility in the field, had civil service status, thus solidifying a greater hold on his position than many of his counterparts in government. After a series of protracted negotiations, including some that involved attorneys from one of Boston's most powerful law firms, Robinson grudgingly agreed to step back into a support role in Counsel's Office.

When Robinson retired in 1980, Robinson wrote a warm note to Anrig, who had pushed him aside several years earlier. He noted "the outstanding contribution you (Anrig) have made to public education in the Commonwealth. You have advanced the Department from complacency to real action" (Robinson 1980). The point of this vignette is that good leaders are able to carry out negative actions on people who work with them and at the same time protect their dignity. It is even possible "to remove most lovingly a person from a job held dear but done poorly" (Author's Recollection). So argued Vermont Governor Richard Snelling, with whom I served as Commissioner of Education in the eighties.

Anrig exhibited another form of right action in people management when he went outside the ranks of the "educator class" in 1975 to hire a Deputy Commissioner. The person who had been Deputy was a beloved old-timer, Tom Curtin, who had served in that post for many years and had as well been Acting Commissioner several times between incumbents. The traditional move in the wake of Curtin's retirement would have been to bring in a seasoned and respected school administrator, someone who could assist the Department in building bridges with local school districts. Given the challenges that the relatively new Commissioner was laying at the feet of local leaders, this may not have been such a bad idea.

Instead, Anrig recommended to the Board the appointment of Michael Daly, a person who had recently decided to retire from a seat in the Massachusetts House of Representatives. He had no credentials as a professional educator. His last post had been as head of the House Education Committee, where among other things, he had been a principal sponsor of the State's special education law, Chapter 766.

The appointment raised eyebrows. First were those of the education community: Daly had little background in schools and almost no formal training as an educator. Next were those of good government advocates: Daly was a "pol", not a professional educator; he would pursue his own political agenda, or worse yet, act with venality, an expected tendency of Massachusetts politicians.

As it turned out, Daly allayed the naysayers' fears once on the job. He wisely chose not to attempt the role of educational professional. Rather he remained a politician, but his political agenda never deviated from that of the Board and Commissioner. Most important, he was exceedingly effective at advancing their cause in halls of the Legislature and within the Governor's Office.

The right path here was for Anrig to make an appointment on the basis of who could best do the job that needed to be done, not who looked the best on credentials traditionally accepted in the field. It is a path that all sorts of organizations are now beginning to pursue because of dire necessity, whereas in previous periods they would agreeably turn to candidates who came across as more palatable to the principal constituents of the organization.

All of Anrig's appointments were not as ingenious and fruitful as Daly's, however. I have already delved into the quagmire that resulted when he appointed someone as chief vocational education administrator, who turned out to be a thief. In addition, he once accomplished the exact opposite of what he had in the case of Michael Daly, to his and every one else's detriment. He appointed a chief of operations for the Department principally because he looked good on paper, a person who had served as Director of Management Services for the New York Stock Exchange. On the job, however, the appointee turned out to be constitutionally unable to make a decision however badly one was needed; in addition he could not move critical papers from his desk to someone else's so they could get on with the task at hand. Instead of the facilitator of operations, he became the bottleneck of operations. To his credit, Anrig acted quickly to remove both from their posts and replaced them with more able administrators.

The Art of Board-CEO Relations

Good people management may be less dramatic than defending the rights of Black and handicapped children, but it is no less important for effective leadership of public affairs. Anrig not only excelled in the ways he handled people who worked for him, he was exceptional in the way he handled the people to whom he himself reported. In fact his innovative management of Board-CEO relations provides us with some of the most useful lessons about building and maintaining constituency support in the public domain.

Fundamental to his thinking about Board-CEO relations was the responsibility he felt he had as a public official to sustain the viability of lay governance in public education. In his own words, "Education is too important to be left solely to educators. . . . the balance between citizen control and professional administration is a strength keeping public education the drive shaft of democracy" (Anrig n.d.).

From conversations I had with him, it was clear how much he relished the notion of working with a Board, particularly one with a rich history and heritage and a commitment to a set of lofty ideals and standards in which he himself believed. This was one of the most compelling aspects of the New York State Commissionership, the positive regard that many citizens had for the historic contributions of the State Board of Regents. Similarly, the origins of the Massachusetts State Board - the landmark Willis-Harrington legislation that initiated it - remained an object of reverence for him throughout his career. He considered it one of his prime responsibilities to help a board with such grounding to build and maintain its stature and integrity.

This disposition on his part - relishing work with a board - is not shared by many CEO's, of either public or private organizations. Frequently they convey the impression that a Board is a necessary evil at best, at worst an encumbrance in the way of getting the job done, a group of prima donnas who do not know the business of the organization, and who thus can not pull themselves together to assist a beleaguered chief who is struggling against difficult odds. In contrast, Anrig saw his Board as a group of citizens who represented an essential counterpoint to his professional expertise. If they could become a true team, the Board could be his strongest defender in a world that was not exactly clamoring to hear the message he was conveying.

Teamwork was critical and Anrig worked with his Board to help its members achieve it. This meant that the Board would have to grow as a corporate body exhibiting ONE mind when needed, in the roles of policy setter, overseer of performance and "court" of final appeal. His insistence on the Board's oneness extended even to the way he referred to the collective membership of this governmental body. When using pronouns in regard to the Board he always used it or its, never them or their.

There were other more binding ways he supported the development of team discipline on the Board. Each of his years in office he developed what he called an operational plan, a document of no more than five pages that laid out very concretely the most important outcomes he and the leadership of the Department sought to achieve in the year ahead. The introduction of a management tool like this was not what was innovative, however. Many good managers employ similar tools.

In Anrig's case, he used the plan as the organizing instrument for his total relationship with the Board. He shaped monthly reports to the Board around the major items in the plan. It became the principal instrument for the Board's annual evaluation of his job performance AND his evaluation of its performance. When the Board approved the plan, it was in effect entering into a performance contract with him as CEO. He would do his part. It would do its part. And in the doing the two together would work out the lines of their relationship, adjusting them as necessary as they went along. Always the benchmarks for the adjustments were the agreed upon tasks as delineated in the operational plan.

Anrig acted out what he knew to be true in a way that few CEO's do. Whether a board becomes an effective deliberative and interactive body - decision-maker, evaluator, advisor, advocate, and buffer - is almost totally dependent on the willingness, desire, guts and sensitivity of its chief executive officer. To paraphrase his own words, for the relationship to work and attain the proper result, both board and executive had to jealously guard the others' prerogatives throughout all that they did together.

From 1973 to 1981 Anrig interacted with the Board intimately, informing it regularly of progress and problems, seeking its guidance and collective judgment, submitting to its regular evaluations of his performance and offering his of its performance at the same time (even when it was uncomfortable to do so). He coached its members to identify and struggle together with policy issues - always placed at the top of an agenda for a given meeting - and he schooled the Board to frame its decisions well and communicate them effectively. He defended the integrity and strength of the Board's role and ultimately guided it into full accountability for its actions.

Actions he took after his first year on the job, 1974, illustrate the unique relationship he sought with his Board. First he submitted his own performance on the job to several hours of rigorous evaluation by the Board. Following this he flipped the coin and offered his evaluation of the Board's performance. From the notes he used for the discussion it is possible to get the gist of this unusual piece of Board-CEO relations. He first reflected on the Board's strengths as perceived in December, 1972, before he took office, and then offered some highlights of the first twelve months.

Then he cited four areas for "examination and continuous self-evaluation":

1. How the Board responds to 'pressure' in areas other than racial balance can be reflective of strength (i.e. openmindedness) or weakness (i.e. avoidance of unpleasantness) . . . ;
2. Distribution of substantive participation in Board meetings by individual members and possible reasons for differences (interest, preparation, deference, etc.) . . . ;
3. Board's capacity to deal with differences openly without feeling offended . . . ; and
4. Self-discipline required of a member of a public corporate body where authority properly is exercised only as part of the corporate body rather than as individuals. (Anrig 1974)

While such interchanges between him and the Board produced an usual degree of corporate discipline, there were also times when the discipline was threatened. Moments like these represent the true test of one's commitment to mutual accountability. A newly appointed State Board member once refused Anrig's invitation to attend a day-long orientation, which had become a firm expectation for those joining this public body. The member's reason was that he did not want the Commissioner to "brainwash" him, and he thought the orientation would detract from his ability to act autonomously. Anrig, joined by the current Board Chair, refused to back down, and the new member came to the orientation (Daly 1994).

At another even more critical juncture, it became apparent that the current Chair of the Board was not maintaining a firm line between CEO and Board prerogative, nor was she exerting good discipline among colleague board members. After a long and difficult conversation with the Commissioner, she promptly submitted a letter resigning as Chair (Daly 1994). Similarly, when another Board member decided to contest in a public meeting a particular personnel action that Anrig had taken, the latter vehemently reasserted and reaffirmed the distinction between policy and operations. Later, after the meeting, he and the Board Chair, took this member aside and offered remediation (Daly 1994).

Anrig took this approach with the Board because the resultant decisions affecting schools, teachers, parents, youth and children would inevitably be better. They would fit more closely the needs of a broader array of ordinary citizens, not just one party or faction. They would have the weight and force of being arrived at collectively, thus offering greater staying power in the inevitable rough and tumble of power politics. Such benefits made it well worth the effort to put his job on the line occasionally, by taking it upon himself to discipline one of his bosses. And whether he was actually endangering his livelihood at these junctures is debatable. The greater likelihood is that these actions coincided with the Board's growing solidity behind him, which was only strengthened more by his willingness to pull selected members back into line.

Lessons on People Management

What are the lessons of the Anrig approach to people management, from relationships with both those who worked with him and those for whom he worked? Number one is that accomplishment of task should govern the conduct of these relationships. The Daly decision and the persistent insertion of and reference to an operational plan reinforce this point. Second is the necessity of having the courage to confront both subordinates and bosses with shortfalls that affect the accomplishment of task. What happened in the case of the thieving vocational administrator, the incompetent chief of operations, and the Board Chair provide fit substantiation.

Next is that it takes time and repetition of right action to build adequate levels of credibility and to inspire enough confidence in others as a public affairs leader. Only a series of positive actions taken over an attenuated period can assist in sustaining a controversial action taken later on. Credibility and confidence can not be created instantaneously, however much they might be needed at a particular moment. The Joe Robinson vignette and the disciplining of wayward board members are cases in point.

Finally, it is possible to take difficult, even extreme and painful, actions as a public affairs leader if one does two things. First is to focus on the tasks at hand, i.e. commit to solving real problems rather than distributing unnecessary blame. Second is to muster and hold close, solid citizen investment in accomplishing the tasks. Anrig did both in composing and garnering the Board's support for his annual operational plans. As a result, the Board became a strong buffer for even the most negative reactions from selected constituents. Witness the fortitude of the Board in dealing with a sitting Attorney General and a newly elected Governor. The two together, an allegiance to task and the cultivation of durable citizen support, made for a powerful combination behind Anrig's agenda for Massachusetts, access to adequate schooling for all in every district of the State.

Chapter 6

REESTABLISHING THE EDUCATIONAL TESTING SERVICE

"I am not a testing expert. My background is that of a consumer of tests. Throughout my career, I have generally felt that there is too much testing in American schools and too much weight placed on test results by the general public. I felt that way before coming to ETS in 1981, I haven't changed since. It surprises people that the head of the largest test development organization in the United States spends most of his time publicly urging that tests be kept in proper perspective, that they be interpreted with care, and that their limitations be recognized by those who use tests as well as those who make them." An assertion Anrig made repeatedly in different forums. This particular excerpt is from a 1985 speech to the National Parent Teachers Association Annual Convention in Washington, D.C.

In 1982, one year after Anrig became President, ETS won the competition for the National Assessment of Educational Progress. Even though it was a multi-million dollar Federal grant, getting the program up and running was largely a hand-to-mouth exercise at the outset. In fact, for the first test administration, a large group of high schoolers were recruited to collate the test books that would be sent out to selected schools across the United States. Because of his personal commitment to the *success of the National Assessment, Anrig continually kept in touch with progress on many fronts. One day he wandered down to the room where the students were, their baseball caps backwards on their heads, laboring away, organizing mounds of paper into piles. For his part Anrig provided the conscripts a short pep talk on the importance of the National Assessment to the future of American Education and their special part in making it a reality. A recollection of Archie Lapointe, Director of the National Assessment, offered during our interview.*

Over forty years from the time Anrig emerged from a family in distress, he assumed the leadership of an organization in distress. The Educational Testing Service was under siege on the outside and divided on the inside. As long-time ETS manager Dave Brodsky said, "the place was experiencing the kind of attacks from outside advocates that many other societal institutions had felt full force in the sixties" (Brodsky 1994). Internally, there was confusion over how to respond to the attacks and dissension on major matters of policy.

The external provocations were multiple. A Ralph Nader-sponsored research study alleged discriminatory and secretive practices by the organization. Called The Reign of ETS: the Corporation That Makes Up Minds, it was receiving substantial publicity and broad discussion. Non-complimentary articles on ETS activities appeared regularly in The New York Times, and a particularly negative essay had just come out in the New Yorker Magazine.

The New York State Legislature had recently enacted a measure calling for truth-in-testing. It required disclosure to the public of previously "secure" test forms for almost all the tests ETS offered in the State. The U.S. Congress was undertaking consideration of a similar measure that would take hold in all the states. The Boston Office of the Federal Trade Commission had completed an inquiry into the impact of coaching on Scholastic Aptitude Test (SAT) scores and concluded that students could raise their scores by as much as thirty points.

ETS is an unusual organization, a hybrid of sorts. It is a not-for-profit entity originally created by three other organizations to do their bidding in test development and administration. The three were the College Board, the American Council on Education, and the Carnegie Foundation for the Advancement of Teaching.   The College Board is a nearly century-old membership organization of hundreds of schools and colleges around the country.   The American Council on Education's membership comprises the overwhelming majority of U.S. universities. The Carnegie Foundation is a major philanthropy.

In some respects ETS looks very much like a business; it has products and services and a bottom line it tracks carefully. In others it operates like an academic institution, with people who resemble college faculty engaged in program development and implementation.   Lacking, however, are students and classrooms. Finally it has the feel of a research center or think tank. Its staff carries out considerable research in areas such as test development, the crafting of educational policy and the evaluation of educational programs.

Inside this complex organization in 1980, there was a growing garrison mentality, a reaction to being attacked from all sides. Wrenching divisiveness crept into the highest ranks as the outside pressures grew. Top managers, instead of pulling together in the face of the onslaught, began to pull apart. Disagreement flared in a number of areas. At the top of the list was whether to hunker down and ride out the attacks or to accede to the swelling demands of the outside critics for greater disclosure of testing tools and fewer discriminatory distinctions in the reported results.

Lack of cohesiveness among those inside the organization was also exacerbating the already bad external situation. Several of the Vice Presidents were not only taking their own separate policy stands, they were increasingly sharing these dissenting views with the outside world. As a result, even more controversy was being stirred up, more outside attacks launched and additional criticism levelled.   Some of the organization's most devoted clients, including the prime one, the College Board, were beginning to wonder if the organization's center would hold (Hanford 1994).

One time ETS Board Chair, John Hennessey, offered his perspective on the situation in 1981 in a letter he wrote to Anrig, then a potential candidate for the ETS presidency:

> Over its thirty three year history, under Presidents Chauncey and Turnbull, ETS has matured into the premier psychometric institution in the country. In the last few years it has also been the focus of important criticism, some of it reflective of the strategic debate over meritocratic vs. egalitarian values in American education and some an understandable consumerist reaction to the very size, power and presumed secrecy of the institution. (Hennessey 1994)

Another commentator, Linda Darling-Hammond, a respected Columbia University researcher on teachers and teaching, was even more straightforward and plain speaking about the situation. She said that when Anrig took over as head of ETS, the organization was "on the verge of becoming a dinosaur because of its lack of openness and its failure to adapt to changing approaches to measurement" (Darling-Hammond 1994).

The plight of ETS in the early eighties was reflected in the increasing number of influential government, education and civil rights leaders who were beginning to regard it as a force for anti-democratic action in education. Whether valid or not, their perception was that the organization was little more than a sorting device, separating out those destined for the Ivy League from the large majority who were destined for lesser institutions or no place at all. ETS-developed tests, they surmised, slated some students for golden futures and left others, particularly people of color, in the wraps of disadvantage contemplating stunted lives (Wilson 1994).

What in fact is testing all about and how and why did Anrig decide to throw himself into the maelstrom that enveloped it in 1980? Reducing lofty notions about what people should know and be able to do to very specific mental probes is the essence of the testing enterprise. After a test developer puts the final touches on an item - a question, problem or exercise that serves as that probe, it joins others in a test booklet or a computer program. The test, however administered, is a succinct rendering of a set of skills or a body of knowledge to be assessed.

People usually take tests at a time in their lives that represents an important personal crossroads, where the stakes are perceived as high. The prospect of getting into the college of one's choice or gaining entry to a profession that one has prepared for years to enter may, in the mind of the test taker, be on the line. In some instances, the stakes associated with testing are indeed as high as they seem; in most, they are really not that high. If high schoolers want to continue their education, they can find secure admission to an appropriate college, even with a low score on the SAT. And eventually, the majority of aspiring professionals pass certifying exams.

Perception and circumstance are what are controlling here. Taking a test is a compelling, and for some, a frightening experience because their estimation of the stakes normally far exceeds the reality. They steadfastly view the consequential effects of test taking in the same way they frame the dangers of flying on airplanes. When the airplane you're riding on jumps and jitters on touchdown, your mind spins out some frightening possibilities. The same happens with test taking. A similar emotional reaction pops to the surface: fear in the face of hovering doom. The overwhelming improbability of a horrible outcome does little to make you feel any less fearful, any more secure.

Anrig went to ETS for a variety of reasons. He had been in the fishbowl of Massachusetts public life for eight years, and it was time to take on some different challenges. A post of national dimension was a logical next step. Testing was also a logical arena for him to enter. Willard Wirtz, a former U.S. Secretary of Labor, was one of those who recommended him for the ETS Presidency. In doing so, Wirtz offered this apt perspective on how Anrig's skills coincided with the challenges of the ETS assignment: "Greg Anrig does one of the best jobs I know of in putting education's ideals to hard labor, which is what testing seems to me to involve" (Wirtz 1980).

For Anrig the ETS job was also another high stakes exercise in public affairs leadership. In Massachusetts, the challenge had been school desegregation and other points of equal access for disenfranchised groups to adequate schooling. At ETS the challenge was realizing the high ideals of education with the very limited tools that had been developed to measure them. In the early eighties the challenge was amplified by the increasing distrust in many quarters of not only the measurement tools but the measurers.

There was yet another complicating factor in the situation. At the same time that public distrust was spreading, the demand from governors and legislators for the goods that only ETS could deliver, i.e. test results, was proliferating. Having launched major education reform efforts in their states, these elected officials saw tests as the best way to prove the worth of these efforts to their electorates.

In 1980 John Hennessey led the ETS Presidential selection committee. There were over 600 applicants for the job, among them 60 present or former college and university presidents and 6 Rhodes Scholars. For many in the education community, a seasoned university president seemed a perfect match for the quasi-academic milieu that predominated at ETS. In fact, Hennessey forthrightly recalled the strong temptation of the selection committee to "rent someone's fame" in light of the hostile environment in which ETS was operating at the time (Hennessey 1994).

Anrig's candidacy convinced the Committee to go in a different direction. As a lead government official, he was no stranger to public controversy, and he had a sound record of managing both himself and the organization he headed in the midst of turmoil. He was also an accomplished educator with deep commitments to improving the quality of schooling and providing all students with equal opportunity to learn and advance.

Simultaneous Challenges

As he had in Massachusetts, Anrig had the dual assignment of defining the major goals of the organization he was heading, while seeking the commitment of staff, clients and constituents to the attainment of these goals. To be more direct, he had to line up the ETS Board and those who worked with him inside the organization. At the same time he had to find some common ground with the customers and critics of the organization and to communicate more effectively with the broader citizenry it was supposed to serve.

In terms that many management analysts use today, he had to outline a vision for the organization and develop a set of strategies for achieving it. One of those strategies had to result in ETS's reclaiming some of the moral high ground it had lost through recent batterings at the hands of outside critics. Another was to get some high quality programming under way. The programming had to be consonant with the vision and resonant with the new moral tone. Its earmarks had to be service, fairness and openness. Finally he had to reflect inside the organization the very same principles that would guide the work of the organization as it provided goods and services on the outside.

These tasks taken together represented a tall order. After all, ETS had grown by 1980 into an organization of several thousand people, in multiple central office sites in New Jersey and regional offices throughout the country. Its operating budget was in the millions, 106 million to be exact. Its roster of institutional clients was in the hundreds. Individual clients, including test takers of such instruments as the Scholastic Aptitude Test (SAT), the Law School Aptitude Test (LSAT), the Graduate Management Aptitude Test (GMAT) and Graduate Record Exam (GRE), were in the millions.

Altering the inclinations of an organization of this size and complexity, beset as it was on all sides, was not going to be easy. One necessary move, according to some organizational analysts, would be to formulate and articulate powerful symbols. Symbols are events, formal statements, personnel actions and diplomatic gestures that send a clear message about organizational direction to large numbers of people who can influence that direction.

Upon taking over as President in 1981, Anrig distributed telling signs, or symbols, of his intended stewardship in every conceivable quarter, as quickly as possible, both inside and outside the organization. He did this in whirlwind fashion, thus laying out the essential lines of his Presidency early on - within the very first months of his tenure in fact. To many observers the whirlwind of activity was almost dizzying. It included work on vision and strategy, the identification of new program initiatives, and the refurbishment of the organization's public image.

To set the stage, he brought a first year draft operational plan to the ETS Board for its consideration and approval, just as he had done with the State Board of Education in Massachusetts. The plan contained the seeds of a vision for ETS. It was that testing should aid teaching and learning and advance equality of educational opportunity for all students. This vision, if embraced by the organization, would at one and the same time draw it back to its roots in some respects and push it in new directions in others.

By the 1980's most of the testing ETS did was used principally by academic institutions and professional organizations to determine the fitness of candidates for admission. Testing as a direct support to the function of education was somewhat secondary. By issuing his operational plan, Anrig began to frame for staff, clients and constituents the organization's purpose as fundamentally educational. When he said, "I am a dyed-in-the-wool educator, and ETS is an educational organization," he was not only citing credentials, he was also clearly indicating a shift of emphasis from the second to the first word of the organization's title.

That students' performance on tests helps assessors and client institutions determine which individuals among many are fit for admission is a given that will likely endure. An equally if not more appropriate use of tests is to assist teachers to teach and students to learn. Reginald Wilson of the American Council on Education dramatized the importance of the distinction, by saying in our interview, "A student will be unlikely to excel if, having emerged from difficult social circumstances, she is doubly penalized by a negative number, in the form of a test result fixed on her head" (Wilson 1994). In contrast to tests reinforcing negative labels, they can in effect convey information about what a student does or does not know to both student and teacher and thus promote continued learning. The net impact is an enhancement of the student's life chances. Thus the rationale for the Anrig vision.

As suggested already, the antecedents of Anrig's vision were evident in the original purposes which ETS was chartered to fulfill in 1948: to create a level playing field for those seeking to move on from high school to college. By making this connection with the root purposes of the organization, Anrig was doing something that many good leaders do, reversing the normal tendency of mature organizations to drift from their commitment to original aims. Effectiveness (work to goal) tends to become less important as organizations age and is replaced with an increasing concern for efficiency (work quickly, at low cost and high return). Put simply, it is easy for leaders to slip into a preoccupation with doing the job right instead of doing the right job.

Investing in National Assessment

There were not many opportunities ready-made that would reinforce the fundamental educational purposes Anrig wanted to impress on ETS. One, however, was "ripe for the picking" as the Anrig presidency was getting underway, the contract for the National Assessment of Educational Progress. In 1982 the Federal Government had declared an open competition to determine which organization would carry out this important function. Until this time the National Assessment had been the preserve of the Education Commission of the States, a national compact representing the fifty states' collective interests in education.

It did not take Anrig long to decide to compete for the grant award. The job of assessing the achievement of American school children was integral to the charter of ETS and it was, he thought, a job ETS could do well (LaPointe 1994). It was also a natural for fulfilling a new vision for ETS. The tests in the National Assessment are intended to measure and report directly on what students know and can do, rather than merely distributing a given population of students into high scoring and low scoring groups.

Put another way, the test reports are not just disembodied numbers. Instead, they portray how many and which kinds of students can do particular tasks well. Significantly, the content of the tasks themselves are made apparent in the reports of the results.

Anrig had voiced great respect for what the Education Commission of the States had done with the National Assessment in the years before. Early on in the contract competition, in fact, he sounded ECS out on the possibility of a joint venture between the two organizations (LaPointe 1994). When this did not appear possible, he set an independent course and weighed into the project with all the mental and physical energy he could muster. Quickly he assembled a proposal writing team that included the most highly qualified thinkers and writers on the ETS staff. Then he hired a nationally recognized figure as potential project director, having him join the team in advance of submitting the ETS proposal. Capping off his commitment, he personally led the ETS team that appeared for a final interview in Washington, and established himself as the "cognizant officer", the one in charge of the effort if the award was made.

According to Archie LaPointe, who has been program director from the start, Anrig read every page of every draft that the writing team put together. "Like a dog with a dishrag" - one of his own "pet" expressions - accurately captures the way Anrig approached the task. Not incidentally, ETS committed $300,000 of its own resources to the process of assembling the team, writing the proposal and making the on-site visits necessary to win the award.

The upshot of his and his staff's efforts was that ETS secured the five-year grant for the National Assessment, an award of almost 4 million per year. ETS itself put in over $1 million of its own money in that first five-year period, above and beyond the $200,000 it had to put in each year as a match to the Federal grant. Subsequent to the first award, ETS secured a second five-year grant, and it was operating under a third five-year award in the form of a contract with the U.S. Department of Education at the time the research for this book was underway (LaPointe 1994).

The National Assessment has become a permanent fixture of operations at ETS. It is central to the organization's sense of itself as being committed to improving the academic achievement of American students in a variety of subjects. The program has issued countless reports on what fourth, eighth and twelfth graders as well as adults know and can do in reading, math, science and several other areas. Most of the reports are well covered by the national and local media. NAEP also serves as a rich source of information for countless research studies that focus on student performance. Increasingly, it is becoming the tool of choice for state school systems to assess their own progress over time and to determine how well they are doing against similarly configured states. A major concern of National Assessment over these past thirteen years has been how students of diverse ethnic, racial and economic backgrounds have progressed and what factors affect their performance.

The National Assessment has served multiple purposes for ETS, well justifying the focused energy Anrig committed to securing it. First, it augmented and diversified the programming capacity of the organization. It brought in new work to do, work that was much in line with the vision that Anrig was articulating. Second, it served the purpose of sending a message to staff, clients and constituents about what the evolving organization stood for. It was a fitting symbol of service, fairness and openness. Third, it enhanced the technical capacity of the organization by compiling a rich data base for research, and by engaging the efforts of talented test experts, researchers and administrators.

Public Positioning of ETS

The securing of NAEP helped a new president accentuate the positive, but he also had much to do to deflect the negative. Even earlier in his presidency, after only two months on the job, Anrig decided to go face-to-face with the largest contingent of ETS's detractors, the viewing public. He accepted an invitation to appear on the Phil Donahue Show. It was a "loaded invitation". The script called for him to respond to the criticisms of two Harvard Professors, Mr. Slack and Mr. Porter. They had just completed a study that showed students could raise their SAT scores significantly through coaching. The study appeared to refute ETS claims that such an outcome was highly unlikely, given that the tests purportedly measured aptitude not achievement. While most of the measurement and policy experts at ETS counseled Anrig against making a public appearance like this so early in his tenure, he decided to do it anyway (Messick 1994).

The show featured a lineup that included Donahue, two expert guests, an antagonist (Anrig), and a "stacked" studio audience. A few were specially recruited to pose particularly nettlesome questions. It was an emotion-filled event. Highlights included a blizzard of statistics from the two intense professors waving studies and reports, along with wafts of anger from several in the studio audience about the unfairness of the tests and the abusive purposes to which educators had been putting the scores. The storm was so intense that even Donahue seemed a bit overwhelmed. At the end of the show he commented, "Dr. Anrig, I take off my hat to you. You have shown a lot of courage to come in here and take a beating like this" (Phil Donahue Show 1981).

Putting aside the matter of who won the psychometric battles that took place on the air - probably the professors did - it was Anrig who prevailed on the political and public relations fronts. He had managed to convey two central impressions that would from then on influence ETS operations. First, ETS was going to open up and receive gracefully, even cheerfully, criticism from all of its constituents. Second, ETS staff were doing a good job and deserved praise for the quality of their work.

Like other leaders, Anrig artfully used outside venues to make a case for internal shifts within the organization he was heading. If leadership entails in part the "ability to frame issues in the public forum" (Drath and Pallus 1994), this was exactly what Anrig did on the Donahue Show. He recast his organization as one that was going to be open to citizen inquiry and criticism. He also publicly agreed to a more realistic concept of aptitude, as much affected by environmental influence and human effort as a fixed and immutable piece of one's genetic endowment. Perhaps most important, he did a reasonably good job of making some pretty complex psychometric issues accessible to ordinary people who were not education experts, but were merely concerned about their children's development.

Attempting to reposition an enormous organization from such a precarious public platform so early in one's tenure might be viewed as unwise. Seeking to address both internal and external audiences simultaneously from that platform was a move that few leaders would attempt. The needs of these two audiences were very different and largely at odds with each other. Outsiders needed to hear the message of openness and willingness to change on the part of ETS. Insiders needed to hear the message, "you're doing a good job." Both messages had to come across effectively, i.e. as sincere and reliable. After all, the climate was laden with suspicion and distrust, and the future of ETS as a sustainable entity was in some doubt. That Anrig was able to reach rather than repel both audiences was a feat in itself.

Adjusting Mainline Programs

As he undertook to quiet public criticism, to add to ETS's program capacity and to shape a new vision, he also had to deal with issues of quality and fairness surrounding the organization's products. Prior to his arrival, his predecessor had led an organization-wide effort to draw up a set of standards for testing quality and fairness. Rather than applying these standards incrementally to current programs, he quickly established a battery of outside audit and review committees, one for every testing program the organization had. He actively sought as members of these committees some of ETS's most ardent critics in the academic and broader educational community. And he asked these committees to look into every corner of existing operations and make the new standards as real as quickly as possible.

Simultaneously, he took this new code of standards for fairness and quality on the road. He testified before Congress and asked the panel looking into testing legislation to accept self-regulation through improved standard setting and stiff outside review as potentially more effective than governmental regulation. He did the same in the state legislatures where the most potentially disabling measures were under consideration. His strategy worked. For the most part Congress and the States agreed to back off in the face of the aggressive self discipline and public reporting that Anrig was proposing and beginning to implement.

Another area of deep concern for the new President was what the organization was doing for the teaching profession. When he looked closely, he saw the National Teachers' Exam (NTE) for which there was widespread disdain in the education community. It did little to advance anybody's thinking about what it meant to be a teacher, including that of the candidates who took the test. The test was, even in the eyes of the testers themselves, an invalid instrument (Darling-Hammond 1994). It needed to be revised. Early in his tenure Anrig made a commitment to do just that. With staff he conceived of a new test called Praxis, one that would not only assess candidates' knowledge of subject matter, but also their performance as designers and implementers of classroom instruction.

As it turned out, the demands of this development effort on teaching assessment were considerably greater than Anrig had originally anticipated. Neither the technical aspects of the performance section of Praxis nor the economics of supporting the project had been worked out successfully at the time the research for this book was being conducted. According to Linda Darling Hammond, ETS had still not managed to excise from its tests some basic "misinterpretations of the nature of teaching and the texture of teacher decision making" (Darling-Hammond 1994). It remains to be seen whether this piece of Anrig's vision for ETS will indeed be put into place alongside some of the others.

If he did not succeed in creating a viable alternative to the National Teachers' Exam in his lifetime, he did manage to become a standard bearer on the national scene for the proper use of teacher tests. For example, when the State of Arkansas sought in the early 80's to use the ETS-owned National Teachers' Exam to assess the capabilities of experienced teachers and to fire incompetent ones, Anrig balked. Ensuing negotiations with state leaders broke down, and Anrig refused to let the test be administered in the state. An interesting side note on this dispute - in the middle of this brewing controversy, Anrig had to go to Little Rock for a conference and found himself at a reception at the Governor's mansion. He introduced himself to Hillary Rodham Clinton, who had headed the blue ribbon panel on Arkansas' educational reforms. It was this panel that recommended the contested use of the NTE. In the receiving line Anrig explained to Hillary who he was. She responded, "I'm glad to meet you, I think" (Author's Recollection).

Later he had to take a similar action in Texas, to disallow the administration of the NTE because it was going to be put to a use similar to the one Arkansas had envisioned. Although Anrig had some strong external support for actions such as the ones he took in these two states, he also had some detractors. Albert Shanker, the outspoken head of the American Federation of Teachers, disagreed with him. Shanker argued that, even if the tests were not designed with a particular use in mind, a more central question was whether the proposed use was proper (Shanker 1995).

Aside from the substantive questions behind these actions, there was little debate among those interviewed that Anrig's steps to prevent the misuse of the NTE represented an unusual seizure of moral high ground. A producer whose revenue depends on selling tests refuses to let a customer have access to a particular test because it would not be used for its declared purpose. This is akin to an automobile dealership screening potential buyers for a history of driving violations. An unlikely scenario!

One possible conclusion - probably correct - is that the head of the world's largest testing organization had major reservations about testing. This was actually an image Anrig coveted, because it allowed him to emphasize what he was first and foremost, an educator. By advocating for the restrained and careful use of the products his organization sold, it also let him stand up unequivocally for product quality and consumer protection. His reasoning was that consumers would prefer to patronize an establishment that displayed product responsibility, particularly when those products could have adverse affects.

Whereas Anrig's struggles inside his own organization to effect a timely replacement of an outmoded teachers' exam may not have been fruitful, he managed to contribute mightily to the advancement of the teaching profession in other ways. One example was the unique notion he had for the establishment of a national board for the certification of high quality teaching professionals. According to Albert Shanker, it was Anrig that came up with the original idea for what later became the National Board for Professional Teaching Standards (Shanker 1995). He saw such a certifying body as a means of securing credibility for the teaching profession with political and business leaders. People of influence had consistently viewed teachers as a group without a set of credible performance standards and the means of making them stick within their professional ranks. The National Board is presently about the business of changing this. By 1994 the Board was issuing its first set of certificates to experienced teachers.

To expert Linda Darling-Hammond, Anrig's ideas on teacher assessment were quite advanced. She said, "the world is still struggling to catch up to his vision." More than anything else, he "provided moral leadership" to an organization that really needed to regain its sense of purpose. "He always took tough stands even when there was a cost to ETS" (Darling-Hammond 1994). There are too few examples of such calculated self-restraint in business, or in education, today.

An Interim Accounting

When the ETS Board was looking for a chief executive in 1980, it was not assessing its needs solely on the basis of impressions and anecdotes. Rather it was informed by a series of confidential interviews that John Hennessey himself had done on behalf of the whole board. He had traveled the country for several months asking over fifty education and government leaders what they thought of ETS as an organization, and how they regarded its products and services.   The picture he compiled from these interviews was not pretty. ETS was seen as remote, inner-directed - even paranoid and secretive, too well-heeled for its own good, and worst of all, acting in a manner antithetical to the democratic ideals that the country was supposed to stand for (Hennessey 1981).

After five years on the job Anrig recommissioned Hennessey to perform the same task he had completed earlier. The results were startling. The fifty or so people interviewed believed that ETS was more open and eager to learn than it had been and that the shift was largely attributable to Anrig. Constituents felt that they could pass through ETS's doors and communicate with the organization. The criticisms that remained, however, were not incidental. ETS, they said, was not yet as active as it should be in aiding the reform of education. The way the organization applied psychometric techniques to educational practice still raised significant questions. Were its tests fair to members of minority groups? Were they reflective of genuinely important intellectual tasks that people should be required to perform? Would ETS be a leader rather than a follower in the emerging movement to assess the outcomes of schooling (Hennessey 1986)?

In his first five years at ETS Anrig had laid down a solid foundation for growth and change. Even though there were still major hurdles, the organization was prepared to tackle the range of substantive issues it was supposed to. Anrig had managed to deflect the self-destructive impulses that top managers were exhibiting when he arrived. He had framed a set of program directions that looked promising.   He had succeeded in reestablishing amenable working relationships with all sectors of the education community. While elected officials and media representatives still kept careful watch on the testers in Princeton, their approach had turned from frenetic harassment to restrained vigilance.

Internal Shifts and Symbols

Much of the foundation Anrig built involved diplomatic work on the outside: in Congressional Hearings; at regularly held meetings of education groups such as teachers, school board members and state education officials; with the media, including reporters and editors; and in one-on-one meetings with key leaders who warranted individual attention. New initiatives like the National Assessment of Educational Progress and Praxis, and partnerships with the Historically Black Colleges and Universities and the Urban League were essential building blocks.

The tensile strength of the foundation, though, came from his paying close attention to the health of the organization itself. There is no more compelling expression of the kind of organizational climate he sought to build than his Christmas time antics. One workday before the holiday - for every single year he served as President - he set out on a marathon trek through every part of the organization within a twenty-five mile radius of his own office. Sometimes he would include one of the regional offices in his itinerary. His purpose was to shake hands, give hugs and wish warm holiday greetings to all in his path. The numbers of people he touched each year exceeded a thousand.

These Christmas visits were legendary events. A favorite venue was the remote site where the millions of test booklets the organization administered were first produced and later shredded. According to site manager Ann Grier, Anrig risked bodily injury one year climbing over palettes and around boxes in his enthusiasm to reach people so as to shake their hand or give them a hug (Grier 1994). Colleague Bob Solomon said Anrig seemed to do this sort of thing to say to all who worked at ETS, "I think of you at this time of year" (Solomon 1994).

Some in the more academic echelons of the organization were, however, less laudatory of their boss's populist approach to management. They were nonetheless as admiring as their blue collar colleagues of the fact that he repeated the ritual every year. In fact, all those I interviewed, even if they seemed restrained in their praise, broke out in a smile when they told the tale of the Christmas juggernaut.

Bearing more the aura of the Grinch than of Santa Claus was the personnel action that set the stage for his handling of ETS's internal affairs. In his first year Anrig eliminated virtually the whole top rung of the hierarchy, letting go of three Senior Vice Presidents. This was a shattering move, certainly for the three who lost their jobs and for others who thought of ETS as offering the same kind of job security as that available at a university. The move also sent a strong signal to the rest of the organization that ETS would be leaner at the top and that infighting within the top ranks was at an end.

Different commentators perceive this stroke quite differently. Some allege that the action did violence to a predominant norm of the organization that promoted open divergency of opinion among inquiring colleagues. The result, they argued, was that the best of the academic culture that had prevailed before Anrig's arrival was destroyed in favor of a repressive political and business ethic. Some also drew the conclusion that Anrig swept the Senior VP ranks clean all at once because of constraints around affirmative action. The argument was that the one Senior VP he really wanted to fire was African American, and the easiest, least controversial way to do it was to get rid of all three of them at once (Anonymous 1994).

Anrig's motivations and the manner in which his mind sifted through the multiple factors that made up this key decision are not reclaimable data at this point. A leader's impetus to act and his related reasoning are almost always lost in the flow that follows a controversial action. The observations and conclusions of participants and onlookers may be helpful, but they are very partial - both meanings intended, and they rarely coincide with each other. There is good reason to believe, however, that Anrig would not have avoided handling the affirmative action aspects of a personnel matter head on rather than indirectly. His whole career offers strong testimony here. In addition, a prima facia case existed for "downsizing" the top ranks of the organization. The charge of his being anti-academic is probably on target, though, given his craving for closure, his bent toward decisiveness, and his appetite for political action.

Equally nettlesome was another internal matter that confronted Anrig early on in his presidency. For several years before his arrival, the organization had seethed with internal dissension over matters of personnel equity. Particularly acute were questions of fairness with regard to the compensation of women and people of color. Through the more academic forms of deliberation that preceded Anrig, organizational leaders had attempted to address the issue by establishing task forces, doing research and analysis, framing recommendations and seeking consensus. But consensus had been impossible to achieve on topics as sensitive as adjusting people's salaries and ensuring the fair appeal of personnel decisions.

Having appointed a personnel equity committee composed of people from all ranks and sectors in the organization, Anrig asked this group to review the situation and report to him directly on pending recommendations. He took their recommendations, and, with startling quickness, implemented them. According to one of the feminist members of the committee, "he did it quickly simply because he said I want it now" (Carlton 1994). Not surprising perhaps, nearly all the ETS employees interviewed for this book cited Anrig's "cutting to the chase" on personnel equity as one of his most significant contributions.

The artful management of symbols is essential to the effectiveness of public affairs leaders. Anrig, as noted, was adept at using symbols for salutary effect. Some he brought forth with genuine spontaneity, others were more planned out ahead of time. One that fits into the latter category was the appointment of Henry Chauncey as President Emeritus. Chauncey had been the Founding President of ETS, and at the time of his emeritus appointment was over eighty. Honoring ETS's past in this highly personal way was a most appropriate and welcome move on the part of a chief executive who was pushing his organization to shift course.

Anrig had a complementary aim in mind when he appointed Janet Bowker an ETS corporate officer. In this instance he was seeking to honor the future more than the past. What made the appointment unusual in ETS's quasi-academic environment was that she had no bachelor's degree. Anrig waved this liability aside because her performance on the job at ETS clearly justified the appointment. In addition to challenging the organization with her appointment, he challenged her with the idea that "you have three years to be able to do anything an officer should be doing." She later said of him, "he saw things in people they could not see in themselves." She also recalled with a chuckle that "whenever he would call me on the phone in the first few years I knew him, I would always stand up, even though I was alone in my office to receive the call" (Bowker 1994).

Impressing upon an organization the need for fair and honorable treatment of employees, past, present and future, may seem only marginally related to engaging outside constituents on issues of fairness, like fairness in testing. They are separate matters and could easily be kept separate. But effective leadership entails an acute awareness of the connection between the inside and the outside of an organization, and how actions taken in one arena reinforce or detract from the impact of actions taken in the other. Anrig was extremely sensitive to this connection and sought continuously to avoid the maleffects of organizational hypocrisy. Fair treatment of people is the same issue, whether it arises "at home or abroad" (O'Toole 1995).

As noted, while some of the symbols of Anrig's leadership were not deliberate, they were no less potent. Confronted with an array of budgetary decisions in his first year, he decided to hold internal budget hearings. These were informal but intense discussions in which line managers presented budget proposals for their units for the following year. One manager, who headed the professional accreditation area, was seeking substantial additional funds for a new computer system. Dave Brodsky was working alongside Anrig at the time to assist in the review of all the budgets. He had worked at ETS since the administration of Henry Chauncey, and had risen to a position of head of business affairs.

After studying the matter of the new computer system, Anrig tentatively decided to offer a go ahead. In private, after the initial discussion with the unit head, Brodsky laid out his strong reservations, which he thought compelling enough to turn Anrig around. They did not, and after the next meeting, Anrig confirmed the go ahead on the purchase. Brodsky followed him into his office and reiterated again why he thought the decision a poor one. He finished with, "I really do not think it is a good decision." Anrig responded, "No shit" (Brodsky 1994).

With this clip of profanity Anrig left little doubt who was in charge. He would listen carefully to perspectives of valued aides, but he would make the final decision. This vignette has an interesting epilogue, though.   As subsequent events demonstrated, the decision to purchase the new computer system was not a sound one. When the signs were clearly pointing that way, Anrig brought the earlier discussion with Brodsky to the surface, and with humor admitted that he had been wrong (Ibid).

Being decisive, being wrong and laughing about it later were important earmarks of Anrig's successful efforts to reestablish ETS as a force for the improvement of education in the U.S. In fact these three factors taken together may have accounted for most of his success. The ability to move quickly on ideas, to admit one's mistakes and to exercise good humor regardless may have freed ETS from its bonds and made room for its reinvigoration.

There are no doubt organizations whose demise would benefit society. Some of its harshest critics in the eighties might have argued that had this been ETS's fate, it would have been a positive outcome all around. The tough truth is that had this happened, we would be scurrying madly to reestablish the capacities it comprises. Because of Anrig we have other challenges, not that one, that we must face.

Chapter 7

CURRENTS OF LEADERSHIP: FRAMES, PHILOSOPHIES, PATHOLOGIES

"I judge people on competence, guts and what they stand for.
. . . Most educators are hard working and dedicated. A few are willing to get out front on the issues and fight against the tide. You not only did this but you sensed the great issues of our time and set the standard for what was right. That's what I call real leadership." - Anrig writing to Joe Nyquist after the New York State Board of Regents fired the latter in 1976 as State Education Commissioner because of his resolute stand on school desegregation.

"If it was good, it was someone else who did it." - Bob Solomon on Anrig's approach to organizational leadership.

Context

The topic of leadership has a tight hold on the way we view life these days. It dominates much of our public discourse, highlighting our yearning for definitive and positive action on our behalves, reflecting the common concern we have for our future prospects and quality of life, and infusing our struggles with the social, ethical and ecological problems that confront us. Leaders of all kinds of organizations in every sector of society, it seems, are beset with the question of whether they have access to adequate leadership. And if they do not, what the appropriate means would be to develop and nurture it.

Heads of corporations are preoccupied with becoming more effective leaders themselves and devising ways for all who work with them to do the same. The common belief is that success, however defined, depends on engendering more leadership capacity not only at the highest hierarchic levels, but on the shop floor as well.

Universities across the country are busy revising their regular list of offerings to include more coursework on leadership development. This is true of almost all professional fields and increasingly the case in the more generalized domain of undergraduate programs. A recent review by the North Carolina-based Center for Creative Leadership provides ample corroboration:

> At one time, a student would have to look in business or education schools to find a course on leadership, and many of the courses were part of the graduate programs. Today, however, undergraduate seminars on leadership are found in departments of psychology, political science, communication, sociology, history, public policy, and women's studies. (Knott and Freeman 1994)

This amplification of attention to the study of leadership extends beyond traditional degree offerings into the more competitive arena of continuing advancement for practicing professionals. In addition, some educational institutions now seek to foster leadership capacity collaboratively with the communities that surround them, thus enriching and broadening their service function. In institutions like Michigan State University and the University of Minnesota, leaders are actually joining with prominent citizens in surrounding communities as equal partners in shaping leadership initiatives to deal with high priority social problems (Author's Recollection).

Many not-for-profit organizations are as much in the hunt for enhanced leadership as their for-profit and educational counterparts. They too are looking for more able executives at the top and greater leadership throughout their ranks. One result of the increased demand is a virtual explosion in the availability of management consultants billing themselves as leadership development specialists. Not only the corporate arena now, but also the not-for-profit sector has as many "helpers" as it can accommodate.

As has been true for a long time, the topic of leadership has a firm place in discussions about the role of government at all levels - local, state, federal, and international. Noted scholars, from James MacGregor Burns to Thomas Cronin, have dedicated their careers to probing the inner recesses of Presidential leadership. Now, in the same way that it has with corporations, the concern about leadership is filtering into the multiple layers that make up the American system of government. It is a rare membership organization of government officials that does not have its own leadership development institute - from school board members to state budget officers to internal revenue service specialists. They are all either suppliers or consumers in the leadership development business, sometimes both simultaneously.

The Center for Creative Leadership, once a fledgling and peripheral entity, is now a flourishing operation active in the mainstream of organizational development efforts worldwide. It is the largest organization in the United States dedicated to research and development on leadership theory and its applications in multiple contexts - with more critical mass on this subject than the university sector. Other university-based centers and not-for-profit entities, some dedicated to leadership development in specialized professional fields, others in areas of advocacy such as women's rights and arts education, are also thriving.

Management and Business sections of bookstores brim with titles on leadership. Such works as <u>The Leadership</u>

Challenge, Choosing to Lead, The Power of Followership, Leadership as an Art, Leadership Without Easy Answers and The Tao of Leadership, offer readers rich scholarly perspective and journalistic commentary on the topic. Of late there is a burst of titles on teamwork, team building and team leadership, including The Wisdom of Teams, Team Fitness, Team Think, Team Talk and Work Teams That Work.

For American society this flowering of concern for leadership comes at the same time that pressures for increased democratization are pushing their way into every corner of our lives - family, work place and world affairs. It also comes at a time when the problems we confront appear more intractable than ever before. Racial and ethnic divisions, substance abuse and addiction, explosive and destructive behavior, environmental and spiritual degradation call out for antidotes.

An Untidy, Emergent Concept

Leadership may be one of the most sought after of all antidotes to our social and ecological ills. But it is neither a sharply defined nor well-delineated concept. Its underlying theories, where they exist, are not grounded in any of the hard sciences. Whereas the social sciences provide some theoretical underpinnings, these could hardly be construed as comprehensive or firm. Rather, leadership is a loosely assembled set of ideas energized by a search for order amidst societal confusion and complexity. Slowly, ever so slowly, it may, however, be gelling into a more formal body of thought informed by organized reflection on unfolding experience.

If it can not yet provide a clear path out of the muddle of our difficulties, the idea of leadership at least provides the impetus to straighten ourselves up, gain purchase and perspective and perceive the potential for order amidst chaos. As unsure as we are of the terrain on which we are moving, with this crude set of tools called leadership, we can scan the horizon, find fellow paddlers and together chart a course that may be positive.

In mulling it over, it is quite predictable that we have turned to a concept that is a bit untidy - a mix of science and spirit - to come to terms with the equally untidy circumstances confronting us. And if untidy has inherent advantages, democracy is fit complement to leadership as a social ordering device. It should be no surprise, therefore, that the more people have exchanged ideas about leadership in the last decade, the more they are construing it in democratic terms.

The brand of leadership we seek now is a variation on that which Tocqueville described over one hundred fifty years ago. A French historian, Tocqueville visited the United States in the early 19th Century, seeking to make sense of American ways. What he found was rampant individualism, softened somewhat by the commitment of many people to informal social organizations, such as church groups and Rotary. The kind of leadership most often practiced in these organizations was the voice of common sense articulated by the ordinary citizen. It derives from impulses present in each and every one of us, impulses that are granted, through democracy, an appropriate and legitimate outlet in the public forum.

As with other major movements in American society, the most central of which is democracy, our present preoccupation with leadership is an exercise in hopefulness. At its foundation is an inevitable leap of faith - so characteristically American, so much in line with what Tocqueville found over one hundred fifty years ago. It goes something like this: even though we can not really fathom the depths of our present condition, our plight and our problems, we will nonetheless refuse to be stayed. Rather, we will get up and grope around for solutions. Collectively we will assume leadership even as we struggle for a better understanding of our situation.

This "Ready! Fire! Aim!" approach is consistent with some of the major defining aspects of the American psyche, an unscientific pragmatism coupled with a strong Puritan work ethic. Again Tocqueville recognized and recounted these very characteristics after he completed his extended visits to this country. They are for many of its inhabitants what makes the social fabric of this country uniquely inspiring and empowering.

So we are at present playing out a drama that we have often in the past, of identifying and defining activist modes to wrestle with the confusing currents in which we find ourselves: with our families, with people of different races, within a quickly changing and hazardous international economy, and within the orb of a decaying physical environment. Our quest for leadership as antidote to the dizzying swirl of quandaries will likely be as boundless, undisciplined and fully contradictory as the quandaries themselves.

It would seem most appropriate in such circumstances to summon up hastily an array of resources to help – <u>people</u> who can lead us out of the wilderness, or the likely <u>set of characteristics</u> which, if manifested by larger numbers of people, could help identify the right route. But as we ride the river of our own inevitable activism in the years ahead, we should attempt to cut against the grain of our natural inclinations. We should instead dedicate as much time as we can to looking around at the terrain and peering back over our shoulder at the ground we have covered. The purpose is to deepen our insight into the possible, to enrich our thinking and to enlighten our actions.

Here's the logic. We want to be someplace else, not here. Headings direct us toward other places. If we want to be in a new place, we need to chart a new course, and it really should be the best course possible. So let's investigate the directions we have already pursued, discover the attributes of the most useful ones, and based on these characteristics, select and head off in our own direction. And when we adjust our bearings appropriately, we will be headed on our way THERE.

A Path of Exploration

Having set the stage for this characteristically American drama of leadership as a set of activist democratic practices, I now present a general definition of leadership. Relatedly I frame how Anrig viewed desirable aspects of leadership. Then I explore some of the newer thinking about leadership as expressed in the literature and soberly assess how well we measure up to its requisites. Specifically, I identify major impediments to our moving forward on our journey toward fulfilling these requisites. In the succeeding chapter, "Lessons From Living Public Affairs Leadership," I seek to capture some of the most profound lessons that Anrig's life has for us. These lessons will come in handy as we struggle to identify the forms of leadership that will allow us to set our course and thus meet our needs in the years ahead.

According to prominent thinkers connected to the Center for Creative Leadership, leadership is best defined as "meaning making in a community of practice." More simply put, leadership is a "process of making sense of what people are doing so that people will understand and be committed" (Drath and Pallus 1994, 2). The decision to take leadership requires of an aspiring leader the "framing of issues in the public forum" and the assumption of responsibility for both action and inaction (Terry 1993).

Leadership is an inherently social activity. For the most part it centers on decision-making about people and resources and management of conflict and communication among people. These elements are present even when those who engage with each other may never meet face-to-face, as with a writer and her audience. Leadership is inherently political and economic as well, in that it almost always involves the distribution of authority and responsibility and the allocation of goods and services among people.

Anrig's Leadership Philosophy

In the terms just outlined Anrig practiced leadership. His actions in the public arena grew out of earnest attempts to make sense of what people were doing so that they would better understand and be committed. His practice of leadership extended to the major educational issues he worked on as well as to the topic of leadership itself. He was, in his own right, an amateur philosopher of leadership, that is to say, a loving thinker on the topic. The word amateur derives from the Latin word for love.

His ten commandments of leadership, recently published by the Washington-based Institute for Educational Leadership, have been widely read and appreciated. They encapsulate his thoughts, and to an unusual extent, characterize the actions he took as a public affairs leader. As such, they represent good grist for our consideration of his contributions both as a leader and a thinker about public affairs leadership. He referred to these commandments, which follow, as "simple-minded but battle-tested views" (<u>Leadership, Anrig's Ten Commandments</u> 1994).

    1. Be yourself. Lead in ways that reflect you. Eventually, people will trust you because of this.

    2. Persevere. Stick to what you have set out to do as long as it is right.

    3. Know your targets and hold yourself accountable to them more than anyone else does. Know what you are trying to accomplish and know how you can tell when you have accomplished it. Create an open system of accountability understood by all.

    4. Don't leave your values at the parking garage. Know what you believe is important, seek it in what you do, and don't settle for less. Stand up and fight for what you believe in.

    5. Live by the Golden Rule in leadership. Treat all others as you want to be treated yourself. Show your interest and concern for the people in your organization, but not in a paternalistic or maternalistic way. Their success is essential for your success.

    6. Don't let power go to your head. Power is granted by others; it is a privilege and a trust. With it comes a disproportionate increase in responsibility.

    7. Attract able colleagues, delegate to them, but use the "hot stove" approach to be sure you know if there is progress toward agreed-upon goals.

    8. Be honest with the public, with the media, with colleagues and with yourself. Don't be afraid to admit that you're wrong.

    9. Have a good sense of humor, and be able to laugh at yourself and what you are doing. Take your work seriously but not yourself.

10. Seek and hold jobs, not solely on the basis of title and salary and authority, but because they enable you to contribute to something you feel is important for others as well as yourself. (Leadership, Anrig's Ten Commandments 1994)

The commandments represent a view of how leaders should behave regardless of the context or circumstances in which they find themselves.   They are the most accessible encapsulation of Anrig's thoughts on leadership, but also the most general. More context-specific is a framework he laid out for a group of leaders in community education.   This framework provides a useful backdrop for the fuller discussion of his vision of effective public affairs leadership that is presented in the next chapter.

Leadership is most important in tough times. No hand wringing. Every crisis is an opportunity to lead. Here are the important 'Do's':
•••• Clarify what you mean (policy)
•••• Establish a focus for leadership/responsibility
•••• Don't wait for others to act - Initiate
•••• Provide help and support
•••• Think collaboration
•••• Think involvement
•••• Practice what you preach

Here are the important 'Don'ts':
•••• Overstate your position. Claim nirvana
•••• Overrely on mandate - by statute or regulation
•••• Wait for money
•••• Get out ahead of yourself - (Rather, think small at least initially - 'a journey of a 1000 miles')
•••• Get into 'turf' battles
•••• Wait for others to initiate
•••• Accept the response 'you can't do that' or 'it can't be done'. (Anrig 1979)

Newer Thinking on Leadership

The current thinking on leadership, manifested in writing done in the last ten years, offers a number of new notions. A central one is that we need to bring about in our society better relationships between positional leaders, i.e. directors of organizational units, and followers, i.e. those who work with positional leaders. In this context "better" means both exhibiting more mutual respect and producing greater results (O'Toole 1995). Dominant is a set of interactions in which positional leaders, or persons of title, and their so-called followers are both bent on behaving as leaders (Lee 1991). In effect, leaders and followers join together and assume responsibility for communicating effectively with each other, taking appropriate initiative and assessing outcomes. This sharing of authority and responsibility is based more on what they know and know how to do, rather than on hierarchical position. In their common endeavor they proportionate among themselves both risks and rewards.

To explicate the dynamics of this new relationship, let me offer what some might view as an extreme example. A person serving as an office clerk used to wait for explicit orders from the boss on which menial tasks to do next, and then carried them out. In contrast, that person today might sit down with the boss once a month and draw up a rough contract for what needs to be done in the next thirty days. Each would lay out expectations and needs for resources and support. Each would agree to take on certain new jobs, i.e. to risk some new ventures. Both would commit to the means of measuring success or failure.

In a month they would meet again, review progress and map out the next month's plan. Whether by title "the leader" or by title "the follower", each would be evidencing important leadership capability, i.e. taking initiative and assuming responsibility. And the result, so goes the theory, is the job at hand would be accomplished faster and better.

Although various leadership theorists take different cuts at the personal and organizational shifts that this new approach will require, there are some common themes. They include *shared leadership, leadership as relationship* and *leadership in community.* First is the idea of shared leadership, of supervisor and supervisee distributing between them the authority and responsibility for a given task or job.

John Nirenberg's The Living Organization highlights this idea and connects it to the idea that follows from it:

> It is not leadership from any one person that is required, it is an aspect of leadership each of us summons from within. In this respect the same qualities we have sought in one person can be found distributed among many people who learn, in community, to exercise their 'leadership' at appropriate moments. This occurs when people are vitally concerned about issues or when executing their responsibilities. Leadership thus becomes a rather fluid concept focusing on those behaviors which propel the work of the group forward. (Nirenberg 1993)

This quotation introduces a second theme, leadership as relationship. This theme expands the idea of shared leadership, but moves away from the attributes, characteristics and inclinations of the individual person who aspires to lead. Instead it focuses on what can happen between people, through such media as participation, partnership and service. It beckons us to envision situations and circumstances, the architecture of which is likely to enrich the possibilities of shared leadership and increase the potential that it will be fruitful. As James O'Toole notes in Leading Change, "to be an effective leader no one can remain a solo operator (even with the aid of television)" (O'Toole 1995).

Finally, there is the theme of leadership in community, that larger set of relationships and organizational contexts where we actually face off against our most difficult and pressing social problems. Here newer notions of leadership point us toward "communities of commitment" (Kofman and Senge 1993). In them there is a marked shift from competitiveness and self-centeredness to cooperation and care for others. These environments bespeak the fulfillment in our daily lives of greater trust and mutual respect, and thereby a much greater capacity for productivity and peacefulness. They are the most positive and sophisticated outcomes of the newer forms of leadership discussed here.

Caveats on Ease of Implementation

The concepts of leadership just presented are attractive, even enticing. They fit well with the way American society has developed to date, founded as it was on strong democratic principles. They are a predictable extension of one of this country's most powerful myths, the myth of Horatio Alger. This story of one person's journey from rags to riches gave weight to the idea that anyone in this country could achieve material success. Even though this more narrow vision has never been realized, we are nonetheless willing to expand the myth to include the intangible benefits of mind, heart and spirit, the deepest recesses where intent and behavior are determined and cast.

But can the concepts be realized, or will they remain lofty and unattainable ideals, like the Alger myth? Assuredly their reality will likely be much more difficult to attain than their formulation. When the stakes are intrinsic, i.e. related to what goes on inside of us as humans, and not extrinsic like the size of our paycheck or the quantity of goods and services we have available to us, democratization will indeed be harder to achieve.

The extent of our success in this bold venture will depend on how well we are able to affect and alter some deep currents that run within us. This will be as daunting a challenge as any we have undertaken. To implement new forms of leadership in our society, the devil will indeed be in the details. It will be in the expressed values contained in single gestures rather than those expressed in well-crafted manifestos, of which there are probably too many anyway. It will be in the nuance that emerges from what is not said in a consequential conversation as well as what is said. It will be in the deflection of ego gratification through a small kindness when all the forces are present to inflate the ego and make the kind gesture an unlikely outcome.

Right now we have in the collected writings of current thinkers on leadership a rough map and a general sense of direction. Denoted on the map are our destination and some potential landmarks, in the form of a new vision of leadership and some attendant goals. There are also some topographic features appearing in the form of coherent and compelling arguments for salutary actions. Roads and rivers show up as the lines of more effectual, productive relationships between positional leaders and followers in organizations, and more broadly in the communities that compose our society. We also know roughly where we want our working relationships with each other to head in order to confront and overcome some of our manifold difficulties. And we have some inkling of the placement of the route markers. But we are still unsure of exactly where we are and what the specific course headings are for this new destination. We are also very short of the paraphernalia, the wherewithal, the equipment that would assist us in getting to the place we think we should be headed.

Our progress is also slowed at present by certain obstacles that deflect us from our goal. We have failed to sight these encumbrances, these rocks in the river that endanger our craft, pushing us to the wrong side of the channel markers, making our progress halting at best. What are these obstacles and what more route-finding equipment do we need to undertake this journey from the reality of our present circumstances to a future reality, an improved state?

A fundamental affliction of the current relationship between followers and leaders is a lack of trust. This is true when talking about positional leaders, or persons of title, as well as persons without titles, individuals who want to be heard on a particular topic so as to influence the course of events. This lack of trust is bred of suspicions on the parts of all, leaders and followers of every stripe. The suspicions are fomented through initial miscommunication and grow as people who aspire to leadership choose to withhold certain crucial information from followers. They do this either because they believe that followers might not have the capacity to act well on the information or because followers would be empowered to act against leaders with the information in hand. In either case they do it to impose their will on followers. Thus the root cause of all mistrust and the reason that change is so difficult to effect in human institutions (O'Toole 1995).

Followers nonetheless seek relevant information because they believe they have a right to it. When rebuffed, either directly or indirectly, they become suspicious of the motives of leaders. Often leaders' actions corroborate followers' fears regarding their motives. Yet leaders continue to hold information unto themselves. And followers continue to seek it more vigorously, even if by surreptitious means such as rumor mills. So it goes, round and round, deeper and deeper, with less and less trust the inevitable result.

Progressive withholding of information is not the only impediment in the way of achieving the benefits of the newer thinking about leadership. Another is that people who aspire to leadership feel that they must take a front-and-center position on the public stage, in the flesh or on camera. They must be seen and heard to be considered a fit spokesperson, which is to say, a leader. Followers for their part are inherently and justifiably suspicious of people who want to be front-and-center all the time. They are fearful of the self-aggrandizing motives of leaders and what those motives are likely to produce: less direct and earnest action by leaders than followers feel the situation warrants.

While these pathologies are bred of garden-variety mistrust, they are fed and reinforced by the hallucination-producing distortions of the modern media. Two people sitting face-to-face across a table can eradicate much misunderstanding, just by getting eye-to-eye, head-to-head and heart-to-heart. This is almost impossible to achieve with the special constraints the camera imposes. The "camera eye" demands a paralyzing brevity, a preoccupation with surface appearances and a thoroughgoing disregard of nuance - a powerful push to *come across as definitive and decisive*, whether one is or is not. All in all the airwaves and the ether are probably the least effective means modern society has developed for restoring and building trust.

Unless we find antidotes for these erosive pathologies we will inevitably be disappointed in attempts to install the newer forms of leadership as ways of addressing the problems that beset us. These forms of leadership are almost totally dependent on trust, the one ingredient of our public relationships that is in such short supply in the present context. And it is the same ingredient most in danger of eradication because of the combined demands and limitations of the devices we have come to depend on to conduct our most important public discussions.

Chapter 8

LESSONS FROM LIVING
PUBLIC AFFAIRS LEADERSHIP

Henry Chauncey was the Founding President of the Educational Testing Service. At the time of my interview with him he was over ninety years old. Mid-way through our conversation, in response to a question about ETS, he paused and said, "Please understand, you really have to wear a hair shirt to be involved with testing." He was referring here to the rough garment made of animal hair that many early Christian penitents wore close to their skin to reflect their commitment to self-sacrifice and denial of bodily pleasure. My immediate response to this provocative comment was, "Did Anrig wear a hair shirt?" After another pause, he countered, "If he did, it was only lightly."

On reflection Mr. Chauncey's comeback offered a most fitting image for the unique brand of leadership that Anrig exhibited in his life. In all his posts he exhibited to a significant extent self-sacrifice, for the benefit of those he worked with and, even more so, for the benefit of the most vulnerable people in our society. But he nearly always did this with great aplomb, ease and humor. He managed somehow to heed his own leadership commandment, to take his work seriously but rarely himself.

A Route to Realizing New Leadership in Public Affairs

Anrig's life offers much useful perspective on public affairs leadership. In great richness and detail it reflects a set of characteristics that must be present if the elements of the new thinking on leadership are to find their way into reality. I elaborate these characteristics here not just to illuminate a path for positional leaders, public or private, in the future. I do it as well to make a catalog of what all of us, leaders and followers alike, will need to exhibit in greater share than we have to date. Let us look back together then over the journey that Anrig made, and we with him, so that as a society we might more successfully complete the one we must now make.

I discuss in the following pages five characteristics of fit public affairs leadership. While described as separate elements, they are in practice intertwined and interdependent. To be an effective leader, a person would have to show strength in each characteristic and balance among all. The five are courage of conviction, principled choosing through wise positioning and felt calling, balanced management of conflict, authentic self-presentation, and commitment to action.

Courage, What Kind of Courage?

Leaders must have courage. Works such as John F. Kennedy's <u>Profiles in Courage</u> are convincing on this point. But what kind of courage, exhibited in what ways and under what circumstances? In the answers to these questions lie greater understanding and more fruitful application. Most of us have observed situations, for example, where people think they are being courageous but they are really not. Rather they have crossed the line from courage to foolhardiness. Their acts turn out on reflection to be the misdirected deeds of bellowers with more guts than brains. As common are situations where the vehemence of the response outweighs by far the consequence or weight of the matter to which it is directed. The image is of a fire hose leveled at a candle flame: "full of sound and fury signifying nothing."   What makes the difference between indulgence in foolhardiness or overkill and the application of genuine courage to a circumstance that warrants it? Surely what is at work is more than sound judgment, simple common sense, good fortune or some combination of all three.

Anrig's life provides some helpful data. It serves to substantiate that true leaders must display more than raw courage.   Rather they must act courageously with great discretion and restraint. They must bring into play the courage of heartfelt convictions, yet apply it thoughtfully to issues of great consequence, and demonstrate it consistently, day by day, over a sustained period.   And they must do all this gracefully, with seeming effortlessness and genuine modesty, out in the open before the eyes of their fellow human beings.

In 1974 the Boston School Committee submitted a plan for the desegregation of the public schools that was demographically flawed. That is to say, the data it provided on various population groups was wrong. Anrig said so in Federal Court, and then gave the Court the correct data. This was at a time when, except for the representatives of the Black plaintiffs, every other party in the case viewed the most minimal cooperation with the Court as a betrayal of community solidarity. Such betrayal deserved not only harsh counter argument but in many instances violent retribution. As previously noted, death threats to public officials who stood on the side of the Federal Court were routine daily occurrences (Lynch 1994; Pressman 1994).

The courage Anrig displayed in the extreme circumstances presented by Boston school desegregation was grounded in strong moral commitments. These were the same commitments as those articulated in the Bill of Rights. His courage was offered quietly yet persistently and articulately in public. Its yield was morally rich even if emotionally costly, for he had to stand nearly alone in the process. His was the only government agency, state or local, that joined the Federal Court as an ally. As Thoreau did <u>against</u> the government in <u>Civil</u>

Disobedience, Anrig did <u>with</u> the government in the Boston case. He took action in a "consequence-producing" context.

The Boston schools crisis presented a set of extraordinary circumstances, full of complexity and controversy, a dramatic backdrop against which to measure the actions of all who were involved. Yet the brand of courage that Anrig exhibited was not particularly extraordinary. It was on the contrary a kind of day-by-day, lunch pail-carrying courage normally exhibited by a supporting rather than a main actor. He merely did what he thought was right - quietly, consistently and forthrightly. Had he done the same in less troubled waters, it might have been viewed as considerably less consequential.

It is lamentable that "ordinary" acts of courage like these have become dangerously rare today. They do not abound in the public forum or the world of commerce, the floor of the U.S. Senate or the conference room of a business firm in mid-Michigan. And their scarcity feeds the pathology of distrust that thrives between leaders and their followers in all sectors and at all levels.

The courageous stand that Anrig took in Boston on behalf of fairness as framed by the 14th Amendment was similar to several he took as ETS President. One of special note was his admission in a national trade journal that he had made a fundamental mistake in judgment on a baseline issue of educational measurement.

The context was a legal action called the Golden Rule case. It involved a dispute between ETS and an Illinois-based insurance company, the Golden Rule Insurance Company. The issue was test construction, deciding which items to include on an insurance certification exam. The heart of the matter was whether the proportion of right answers on the test should match the proportion of ethnic group representation in society. Given that twenty percent of the population is African-American, for example, should the test include only those items that roughly twenty percent of the African-Americans taking the field test are able to answer correctly? The use of such a criterion for item selection would increase the likelihood that the composition of the group passing the test would mirror society's ethnic make-up.

Anrig's eventual acquiescence with the criterion as stated above formed the basis of the settlement of this legal action, which had been pending for several years before he became President. His intent was to settle the case and confine the effects of the criterion to the particular area in which the case had been brought, insurance certification. Unfortunately this was an unrealistic expectation. Other professional and academic constituencies demanded application of the criterion to their certifying tests and this was beginning to happen (von Mayrhauser 1994). Agreeing with ETS scientists that what might be appropriate for the insurance business was not necessarily fitting for other fields, Anrig resolved that the position he took on Golden Rule had to be altered. He decided to accomplish this by issuing a formal public retraction. In line with his wishes it appeared as a front page article in the bulletin of the American Psychological Association (APA Monitor 1987).

Disagreement still lingers among measurement experts about the validity and appropriateness of the criterion with which Anrig concurred to settle a law suit (Cole 1994). Similarly there is no strong unanimity of opinion behind the opposite position articulated in Anrig's retraction - published on the front page of the APA Monitor. That position was that test items should be selected principally on the basis of whether they accurately measure the knowledge or skill at issue. And if the result is that the percentage of right answerers fails to match the proportion of different ethnic groups in society, then so be it.

From the perspective of one concerned with framing leadership concepts, the most telling feature of the episode is how direct, unequivocal and clear Anrig was in making the retraction. As startling is that he chose to convey it with such pinpoint accuracy to an audience likely to be most critical of whatever position he took. It is rare for a person in a public position to offer an outright retraction. It is rarer yet to call it to the attention of one's most vigilant and vigorous critics. The usual mode is to seek back page coverage, phrase the retraction in guarded language, sandwich it between phrases defending the original move as logical and done in good faith, and invoke a host of caveats.

While considerable controversy remains over the issues in the Golden Rule case, little exists with regard to Anrig's leadership behavior. A person in a public position serves well - and is served well - when on occasion he takes an unambiguous stance, without condition, without excuse, and relays that stance to those most concerned about the issue. If, in his view, he made a mistake that had a negative impact on the work he was supervising, then he owed it to himself and those working with him to take strong corrective action.

Sound public affairs leadership requires careful reflection on the circumstances in which one finds oneself, a recognition of one's own part in creating those circumstances, acknowledgment of the extent of one's responsibility, and the application of right action. As a society we have to take steps now to regrow this kind of leadership timber if we want a sturdy craft for the next stages of our own socio-cultural journey.

Positioning of Self to Serve Societal Needs

Courage, born of conviction and deftly and quietly applied to consequential circumstances over sustained periods, determines in part who should assume leadership in public affairs. But leadership involves more than this kind of courage. Of equal importance is a person's ability to attain a platform upon which to act on values, a place where right action can be carried out. The key dynamic here involves the application of moral tenet to the events at hand in the context of the time and place that frame those events.

Anrig's life demonstrates the value of positioning. He positioned himself well for accomplishment and for contribution. One might conclude from this that the idea is simply to be in the right place at the right time. This would not be an unwarranted conclusion; it is one with which we are familiar and comfortable. Much of the rightness of place and time is attributable to luck, some to the choices that we make. These choices are thought of mostly as matters of strategy, a set of careful calculations mixing self interest with the interests of others. And most of the time it is expected that self interest will take precedence over the interests of others. Furthermore, in a democracy people should and will position themselves advantageously, so there is little need to be careful of others. This is just the way it is - and probably should be. Right?

Wrong! The reasons are somewhat complicated. Eastern philosophy may spark initial understanding.

> There are places in nature that can give people great power, but the character of the individual determines whether the power is used for war or peace. It is not enough to struggle for vantage points. Position must be used with wisdom. (Deng Ming-Dao 1992, #249)

Anrig's accomplishments and contributions were undoubtedly attributable to definite acts of courage. They were also due to persistent and principled choosing on his part. This involved melding the attainment of social ends with the fulfillment of his own ego needs. He expressed this kind of choosing most profoundly when confronted with alternatives that affected the course of his own professional and personal life. He expressed it as well when confronted with consequential decisions within the issue areas of greatest concern to him, teaching and learning, civil rights, the balance of governmental authority and assessment.

I have discussed earlier the decisions he made regarding turns in his own career. Of note was how intimately connected those turns were to the larger educational and social ideas to which he was committed. Few of these decisions were predominantly self-serving or based solely on ego gratification. This is not to say that only selfless causes dominated his thinking at the time of key life decisions. Much as there is to admire about Anrig, he would not have been a good nominee for sainthood. Nonetheless, it is fair to say that there was an unusual degree of attention in his decision-making to what would benefit others, not just himself.

For example, when he chose to seek the Massachusetts job, he had a clear vision of what state leadership could mean to improving the quality of education in the 70's and 80's. He was equally clear about the assets he could bring to this context. The

ETS post, in contrast to the Massachusetts assignment, had the potential for significant material gain for him and his family. Yet his foremost interest in it centered on the role of testing and assessment in the forging of a new set of relationships in education - not only among teachers, parents and students, but also among federal, state and local entities. He reflected this determination by being perpetually resistant to displays of lavishness while at ETS. In fact he repeatedly evidenced embarrassment at even the most inconsequential and well deserved perquisites of office (Horne 1994).

The brand of choosing I have described here is one that is strongly grounded in the notion of a "calling", a concept that has become somewhat outmoded in contemporary society. A calling is born of the connection between how one spends one's working hours and a higher set of considerations, religious or secular, i.e. a cause. In the absence of the primacy of calling, the consistent display of generative leadership is impossible. This is true whether one is a lead educator, a volunteer for Alanon, or a manager of systems maintenance at IBM. Anrig's calling was equality of educational opportunity and improved teaching and learning for children in the nation's classrooms. For others there are different aims, but in almost all instances, calling is defined by an affirmative response to the question, "Am I my brother's keeper?" Perhaps it is the fate of fellow human beings around the table at an Alanon session or the continuing productive employment of one's co-workers in a sub-division of a computer manufacturer. The nature of the calling is less important than its presence and force. Calling should have a first-rung status in decision making regarding one's own life as well as others'.

These ideas - about courage of conviction and principled choosing - have a decidedly old fashioned aura. They draw directly on 19th century American archetypes, and include such elements as: the connection of one's actions to a set of moral principles to which one is called; a willingness to take such actions in public forums where others' reactions might be adverse; the likelihood of incurring public censure or even the infliction of psychological or physical harm because of one's public positions; and the expectation that actions will be the outcome of decisions where one's own needs are not only balanced against others but are frequently submerged in them.

Furthermore, many of these ideas and qualities, viewed in the contemporary context, have a distinctly female orientation to them. A century ago they would likely have been viewed as much the province of men as of women. In any case, elements like the ones mentioned in the last paragraph are hardly part of the ebb and flow of public affairs today. They are not the distinguishing marks of late twentieth century leaders. They are certainly not the most telling aspects of twentieth century forms of leadership as practiced principally by men. Present day modes involve much less attachment to calling, more preoccupation with gamesmanship, strategy and tactics, artful positioning and presentation of attractive images. Such contemporary approaches, when not undertaken for the enhancement of self-esteem, are used to gain position, power or lucre. They are reflective of a moral code that is less strict and a sense of commitment that involves much less reciprocity, much less give and take. Rightness acted out publicly is rare. Much more predominant in public affairs is the couched phrase, the careful statement, the planted story.

Judge Garrity presided for twenty years over one of the nation's most controversial urban school desegregation cases. He commented toward the end that he much preferred dealing with the local school leaders who were in office early on in the conflict. The advantage they had over their successors was that they were explicit about their biases. Those who came later were subtle, their intent cloaked, their motivations difficult to assay (Garrity 1994). The aging judge seemed to be longing for an explicitness and forthrightness in public affairs, even if outright racism was the point of view being aired.

Whether leadership attributes like Anrig's ever dominated the conduct of our public affairs is actually less important than the question of whether we need them now. At this juncture, in the wake of events like the O.J. Simpson verdict, the need appears to be especially compelling. The ways and means of building fundamental trust between groups, mired as they are in deep mutual suspicion, seem somewhat far from our grasp.

Seeking Out and Deflecting Conflict

Disabling conflict that inhibits positive action is where we find ourselves on many fronts. Racial division is perhaps the best example. Analysts agree that a person who aspires to leadership must be able to manage conflict. For some, this amounts to "managing" it out of existence, taking whatever steps are necessary to achieve harmony, even if paper thin and temporary, in the face of conflict. For others, it entails what Harry Truman had in mind when he contemplated his kitchen - learn to like the heat or get out. All in all Americans seem somewhat lost when it comes to dealing with conflict. We are suspended precariously between the more accepted dog-eat-dog, Darwinian reality and the more halcyon prospect of cooperative community offered up by some of the latest writers on leadership.

Is there any way of drawing together the pull of these poles, of seeing through the confusing and ambiguous muddle and defining more clearly the responsibility that a leader has for handling conflict? There are useful lessons for us in the details of the life examined here. Anrig practiced ego deflection to an unusual degree in his public life - and probably in his private life as well. It might be fair to say in fact that he behaved with friends, colleagues, bosses and enemies more like a woman than a man, at least as far as traditional gender roles are construed today. Suppressing one's own needs when confronted with others is a function that has traditionally been reserved for women in our society. Likewise, seeing the potential for cooperation in conflict and acting to make it real are roles normally assumed by women.

Former Boston Globe journalist Muriel Cohen, without referring to gender roles necessarily, saw Anrig's way of handling conflict as follows. He sought out spots of acute social conflict, she said, because he saw them as places where he could get things done, i.e. make a contribution on the issues he cared about. But he never seemed to do it because he relished conflict. She noted that in the middle of heated verbal conflict, he would block, blunt and dodge the intensity and force of it with whatever means he could summon - usually a combination of self-deprecating humor, artful deflection of others' hostility and continuous exhortation for all to be of good will (Cohen 1994).

It was as if he sought out a fight and then asked if the combatants might want to consider being somewhat more gentle with each other. Perhaps backing off would make sense, or at least showing more respect for each other, or at the very least not taking each other so seriously. Any of these, he seemed to wager, could assist in dealing better with the multitude of differences that caused division, making it more possible to find common ground and get on with the task at hand.

Having one mindset with regard to selecting battles and stepping up to them, and a different one about the rules of engagement in conflict, is integral to effective leadership. The first state of mind is governed by the courage of convictions, principled choosing and the primacy of calling. The second is governed by a commitment to preserving human dignity at all costs, an aversion to emotional and physical violence, and a willingness to rein in one's own ego for the sake of the collective good. The nurturance of peace, both in the heat of battle and beyond, where deep differences likely fester, is imperative.

In political arenas, i.e. life, people clash over basic values. This is inevitable. Compensating for the discomfort of these exchanges is the potential their resolution offers for achieving progress in human affairs on matters of fundamental concern. But once parties are fully engaged in conflict with each other and they commit to see the struggle through, they have a superordinate obligation to summon up the inclination to treat each other with the utmost respect, care and gentleness.

This all sounds Taoist or Confucian - an acknowledgment of the yin and yang, an acceptance of ultimate contradictions, a commitment to achieve delicate balances, a willingness to unite the best of the masculine and the best of the feminine in all of our dealings with each other. Yet it is these very combinations that could help us attain some of the goals that newer forms of leadership espouse, for example, the establishment of "communities of commitment". The move to preserve life by respectfully, even cheerfully, embracing conflict that may threaten it, is the most promising means available to us as we labor to address the difficult problems before us.   Perhaps "wearing a hair shirt lightly," as Anrig did so often and with such flare, captures the requisite contradiction that is essential to making progress.

Authentic Self-Presentation for Good Purpose

So far we have examined three ingredients of effective leadership - courage born of conviction, the act of principled choosing through positioning and calling, and refined ways of approaching and engaging the inevitable conflict in human affairs. I turn now to one of the most often discussed yet difficult to grasp characteristics of effective public affairs leadership - openness and honesty.

For most these two words conjure up visions of colleagues who are willing to share some personal material about themselves with others. One way may be to share openly with others a set of troubling personal circumstances or, on a slightly more lofty level, a felt existential dilemma.   Current thinking seems to be that doing things this way shows that a person has emerged from denial and rejection to acceptance and integration of affliction. Such personal revelation is seen in many quarters as prerequisite to effective leadership of one's peers. The literature and lore around sensitivity training provides ample substantiation for this point of view.

If this were the standard, Anrig would have come up very short indeed. He was an extraordinarily private person, so much so that a few of his co-workers wondered openly in interviews if he had a hidden life that no one knew about. It would not have been hard to achieve a consensus among many who worked with him closely that he was in many ways repressed and therefore not fully self-actualized in a modern sense. A "New Age" figure he was not.

That he was not totally repressed would have been corroborated by those who were exposed to his anger. At times, particularly those in which the welfare of a family member or the application of a central value was at stake, he did not keep his anger under wraps. Instead he let it out, usually in controlled bursts accompanied by generous amounts of profanity. Such emotional outbursts were the clearest evidence of his vulnerability. Luckily for those around him the episodes were relatively rare, and confined to private conversations - although in his last few years at ETS he became more openly testy more often (Horne 1994).

In terms of the expectations we hold today for our leaders' openness and honesty, Anrig might appear wanting on some important dimensions. From his life story emanates almost no copy fit for <u>People Magazine</u>. There were no juicy tidbits, no sexual encounters on the sly, no shameful family secrets, no boondoggles on the company tab, not even the occasional glamorous outing.   How great a contrast, though, between the way he presented himself personally and the way he presented himself on behalf of the organizations he led. He was deeply committed to organizational openness and honesty, and steadfast in effecting and preserving it.   In the course of his professional career he accomplished rather remarkable feats on these fronts. He was a disciplined, some might say zealous, practitioner of full disclosure to constituents and the media, even to the occasional muckraker and the omnipresent auditor.

A long career as a journalist made Muriel Cohen a chary dispenser of praise for public officials' openness to outside scrutiny.   But she called Anrig's commitment to disclosure unusually strong. Her only demur was that if he held back information, it was more an act of omission than commission. One of her clearest recollections was the surprising degree of disclosure he evidenced during the vocational education scandal which had been visited on him when he was Massachusetts Education Commissioner. On reflection she insisted that she could not recall an instance of greater self and organizational revelation by a public official than that which he offered at the time the scandal was unfolding (Cohen 1994).

When Anrig went to ETS, the presumed, and at times well- practiced, secrecy of the organization was one of the most steadfast "monkeys on its back". In his first year he quickly carried out an aggressive strategy of inviting into the organization some of its harshest critics to review the substance of its work. Five years into his term as President he repeated a step his

Board of Trustees had taken when it was embarking on the search that resulted in his appointment. He asked the Board to dispatch one of its own, a seasoned interviewer, to survey a range of constituents on how they regarded ETS. He wanted to know if there was any perceptible change in constituents' assessments of the organization from the time of the previous survey and what ETS might do to address their continuing concerns. When the survey results came back he shared them openly with the Board. Actions like these probably did as much as any internal overhaul or external publicity campaign to restore the organization to vital functioning in the 80's.

Is it possible that some of our present calculations about what makes for effective leadership are off the mark, particularly on the matter of the appropriate balance between personal honesty and openness and organizational honesty and openness? Perhaps we are counting too much on personal openness to offset the ill effects of the mistrust that besets our organizational lives. Perhaps we should review the benefits of organizational openness per se and not assume that personal openness is an adequate substitute.

This is an era of proliferating personal disclosure amid rampant public mistrust. Yet it is also an era in which, for good or ill, organizational dynamics dominate our lives. It is a time too when electronic media are omnipresent, in and of themselves causing profound distortions in our public interactions. The effective functioning of our society depends to a great extent on finer distinctions and greater clarity with regard to what we value when it comes to openness and honesty.

In sum, the genre of personal openness and honesty to which we have become attached may indeed have more value for popular media displays and cocktail party conversations than for consequential working relationships in organizations and within society as a whole. Because it is more revealing the genre may seem more authentic. In reality it may be less so as it is not leavened with a genuine commitment to social welfare.

If not reflected in our formal organizational behavior, personal openness and honesty will gain us little in coming to grips with difficult social problems. How our organizations behave is in the hands of positional leaders and those who lead from within. Anrig's persona was genuinely stretched between the requisites of self-presentation and community well being. This special brand of authenticity is one we should determine important enough to be replicated.

Doing

This chapter has advanced the notion that leadership attributes such as courage or openness and honesty need careful elaboration and placement in context. They are not absolutes, and treating them as such in the frame of the new thinking and writing about leadership may be more harmful than helpful. I turn now to an idea that is often passed over in discussions about leadership, the simple notion of doing.

The popular slogan from a Nike shoe ad, "Just Do It!" describes well the move that Anrig made in most of his professional career. "When in doubt, attack" was a crude maxim he applied to many of the circumstances in which he found himself. Granted, there were several occasions when "not doing it" might have been a better move for him. One of note was the deadline he established and reinforced rigidly in his last years at ETS regarding the development of the new teacher performance tests, Praxis. The successor to the National Teachers' Exam, Praxis was intended to be a product of which all at ETS and in the education community could be proud. But complexity and cost stood in the way, and neither the deadline nor the standard of quality was met.

For the most part, though, his tendency toward rapid engagement and resolution, usually for the express purpose of implementing pieces of legislation or board-generated plans, stood him and those he served in good stead. For example, he took a series of equal opportunity laws that the Massachusetts Legislature had passed and made them come to life in the schools and communities of the Commonwealth in the short space of five years. Granted, behind the "just do it" slogan were important leadership capacities that came into play in mutually reinforcing ways: an ability to incorporate into his own mental frame the vision that these laws embodied; systems design skills to formulate and carry out feasible plans each step of the way; people skills to draw allies and disarm opponents; and an iron will combined with an extreme drive to get the job done.

Similarly, at ETS, he packaged the set of standards on testing fairness and quality that his predecessor had developed and took them on the road, to every constituency with an "ax to grind" about testing. He advanced them with as much vigor and enthusiasm as he could in the public forum - in Congressional and State Legislative Hearings and in the print and electronic media, including talk shows. He demanded their implementation in the workings of his own organization and sought the perspective and advice of outside experts on testing - many of them avowed critics of ETS - to ensure their wise application.

We have many problems today that befuddle and at times stymie us. Certainly we can not start attacking them willy nilly, dispersing our limited energies all over the social landscape. We can not really "just do it!" We can, however, take a page from Anrig's book. When we have a sense of direction and can chart a course, it is probably time to join together and "start paddling like hell." There is more to lose from doing little or nothing than from seeking out the springs of action and unloosing them. W.H. Murray, reflecting on one of Goethe's couplets, said it well, ". . . the moment one definitely commits oneself, then Providence moves too. . . . Boldness has genius, power and magic in it" (Readings from the Hurricane Island Outward Bound School n.d.).

The connection between persons and issues in the public forum is robustly interactive, person to issue and issue to person. What we DO on issues changes them and they us. If we lay back in the face of the daunting presence of difficult issues, then they will confound us and we will lose our hold. In some deep sense this progressive slipping may be what is occurring today. It will take a lot of DOING to recover the proper balance. Anrig's commitment to action is something we should borrow and use frequently.

Let me review the lessons of this chapter. A leader must infuse a commitment to act with authentic self-presentation, well balanced between self-interests and social needs. A leader must ground actions in principled choosing, kept strong through a firm sense of calling and maintained through wise positioning. As these ingredients actively combine, conflict will inevitably arise. For forward movement to occur a leader must accept this conflict as integral to public affairs leadership and coax the contending parties to a higher plateau of resolution, preserving throughout the dignity of all.

Chapter 9

LEADERSHIP LESSONS
FROM WORKING THE ISSUES

Reflection: is it possible to sum up the contributions of a person's life to the development of the social issues on which he worked? Is it possible to do this with a level of insight that will allow readers to draw some conclusions about the directions the country ought to pursue in the days ahead? Questions of this sort preoccupied me as I laid plans for these concluding formulations. After considerable mulling I slipped almost effortlessly into a different perspective altogether on the questions. I should do merely what Anrig sought to do throughout his professional career: make the complexities of educational policy making as uncomplicated as possible so that ordinary citizens might be more empowered to make decisions about them. This, after all, was one of his major commitments in public affairs leadership. From a single serious conversation with him, one could sense his disdain for artificial complexities and the educational jargon they are wrapped in. He could barely tolerate these in academic institutions where they are the perpetual stock in trade. He could not abide them at all in public forums like legislative hearings or board meetings. The people who attended these sessions wanted access to decision making but saw their lack of professional credentials as a deterrent. In the spirit Anrig brought to educational policy making I offer this wrap up. It seems a most fitting way to reinforce aspects of thinking and deliberating he held dear, simplicity and accessibility.

     Public transactions regarding policy - these were Anrig's milieu and his metier, his working environment as well as his work. They formed the points of intersection between people and issues that comprise what public affairs is all about. Policy for Anrig was not a disembodied set of rules and guidelines. Rather it was society's life blood, a dynamic flow that led to a better future. It was, in a more personal sense, his opportunity for public affairs leadership, his vehicle or instrument for making contributions to a society whose institutions had supplied him with the nurturance that he needed to grow.

     But what is policy and who makes it and how? Even when formulated and issued in the form of new law, agency directive, labor-management agreement or just plain public statement, does it have much of an impact? Does it really affect what teachers, counselors, administrators, lay leaders and parents do as they go about the daily tasks of educating children and youth in schools, in community centers, in homes?

     Anrig paddled away in the streams of educational policy for three decades. What in sum and substance was his work all about? Did it make any difference in the educational experiences of children and youth in this country? Even if it did not make an immediate difference, does what he did, said and stood for hold promise for addressing the educational challenges we will face in the future? What in effect is there for us to learn from the plotting and plodding he engaged in from the mid-sixties to the mid-nineties - in Washington, D.C., Massachusetts and Princeton, NJ?

     Policy, some analysts argue, can be best grasped by looking closely at what people actually do and deriving a set of prescriptions from those actions. It is as simple as saying, "I am going to look at what you do, take a step back from it and infer the sort of guidance you might have received from somebody else or from yourself that led you to do it." What one gleans from such an exercise is a pretty clear sense of the policy that obtains. This approach is exactly what John Goodlad did in his book, A Place

Called School, for example.   He undertook an exhaustive examination of what teachers and others did in classrooms and derived real - as opposed to espoused - educational policy from it.

The approach just outlined reinforces the belief, perhaps true, that there is no stronger force in determining policy than the status quo, the way things are and have been for a while. It is also driven in part by a frustration that much of the verbiage that so-called policy makers issue in one form or another falls on deaf ears anyway and rarely finds its way into what professionals and those associated with them do.

The overwhelming power of the status quo in public affairs is driven home for us all the time. It certainly came home for me early in my tenure as Education Commissioner in Vermont. The time was 1983, the place a legislative hearing room in the Capitol in Montpelier. With the strong support of the Governor I had proposed a comprehensive early education program for all children in the State, age three to grade three.   The Appropriations Committee of the House of Representatives was considering the measure and had asked me to testify on it. After listening to me for only a few minutes, one of the older members of the committee interrupted me, reared back in his chair and said what he thought was abundantly obvious to all present, "We can't do that; it's new." In effect, end of discussion, next item!   My jaw fell open as the room fell totally silent. I was done, or rather done for. Herein lay strong verification of the power of the status quo in the face of cogent arguments to the contrary.

Existing policy may best be grasped by scrutinizing existing practice, but it does not necessarily follow that what one should be doing is necessarily what one is doing now. The main reason is that everyone would stay tethered to conditions of practice as they are in all public and private institutions. At best, practice might improve gradually over very long periods of time. With a vast array of social, economic and ecological problems breathing down our necks, beckoning us to devise bold new approaches and take enlightened action, this "let things be" approach might be somewhat hazardous at the moment.

Although there is little evidence on the matter, Anrig probably would not have contested the analytic value of discerning policy from a rigorous review of existing practice. At the same time his career stands as compelling testimony to the idea that the role of leaders in a democracy is to talk and act so as to move other people to consider changing their beliefs and attitudes. In turn, these listeners might then be willing to change what they are doing. If they work in a school or have a position in the community that affects what goes on in a school - a most important venue for educational policy - the change would be with the ways they interact with children.

Policy directives are tossed out into the public arena in the form of federal or state statute, court decision, local ordinance, agency rule to interpret law, collective bargaining agreement, or incentive measure carrying dollars or other benefits (Elmore and McLaughlin 1988). Even if their intent is clear with words that are relatively concrete, the consequences or effects of these measures are bound to be uncertain. For their language is filtered through the incredibly complex sieve of human behavior - actions, reactions and interactions. People have different needs and perspectives, and therefore are likely to act in different ways or not act at all when confronted with policy. So one way or the other, either in the deciphering or the implementing, there is likely to be significant dilution of or deviation from the initial intentions.

The result is that when policy is issued it rarely takes hold firmly, even if large amounts of money go along with it. Instead it hovers over the moves and meanderings of a large number of people for a considerable period of time. At some times, in some places, it seems to take hold. At other times, in other places, it remains peripheral to what is actually happening. It is also possible in some instances that the intended coverage of the policy is narrow, but when implemented it becomes quite broad. In other instances the reverse turns out to be the case - a policy of extensive reach falls very short in its actual grasp.

This latter effect has seemed the inevitable fate of policy designed to spur innovation in schools. In the last thirty years, there have been several heralded efforts at the national level to foster school innovation. In the mid-sixties the innovative projects section, Title III, of the landmark Elementary and Secondary Education Act, in the seventies the Experimental

Schools Program, in the early nineties the New American Schools Corporation - all were intended to initiate a redesign, perhaps even an overhaul, of schools as we know them. None has.

Policy is a very blunt - and therefore very imperfect - instrument for leadership in public affairs. Even when a person or group is genuinely adept at formulating it, at broadcasting it, at drawing the appropriate people's attention to it, and at asking, nudging or requiring them to act on it, the chances of its actually being incorporated into people's day-to-day activities is relatively slight at best.

If the slope of implementation following the act of policy making is somewhat slippery at the issuing stage, it becomes a treacherous, ice-covered incline shortly thereafter. Soon after passage or issuance of a policy a series of glaring shortfalls usually appear:

•••• Since the words of the policy almost always leave ample room for interpretation, constituents are frequently able to fit what they have been doing for the last several years within the frame of the change advocated. They declare full compliance and do exactly what they have been doing in the past, which is actually inconsistent with what the policy calls for. A classic example of how this unfolds in education is as follows: a hypothetical teacher says, "There is a new policy in this district on cooperative learning, kids working with each other in small groups to organize and carry out tasks. I have been doing this for years." The actuality is that she has been doing some of it in some fashion, but nothing like what the policy really calls for.

•••• People who write policy often struggle mightily with questions of eligibility, of coverage - which groups or individuals should be affected, which should receive benefits. Policy setters rarely succeed to the extent they wish, often undershooting the target, more often overshooting. The size and diversity of the group that claims eligibility - quite legitimately in the terms of the policy - can serve to undercut its original intent. For example, a transitional bilingual education measure is passed as a way of beginning to meet the needs of the Spanish-speaking population of a given jurisdiction. The bill has a modest appropriation to provide additional resources to school districts that will have to provide special services. Soon a host of other groups, for whom English is a second language, legitimately demand the benefits the policy offers. What began as a benevolent, narrowly targeted and modestly funded effort turns into a highly competitive, desperately underfunded program fraught with frustrating bureaucratic obstacles. The unanticipated consequence of having more eligible constituents than one bargained for causes disarray. Policy makers need to redraw and implementors reshape what they are doing. Neither winds up serving the aims originally advanced.

•••• Policy, even when targeted to a particular purpose or group, is supposed to respect the needs of all segments of the population. The reality is that all policies offer tough trade-offs. What's good for the goose may in fact not be good for the gander. Usually one segment of the population is advantaged over others. It is a plain impossibility to attend to the multitude of special situations that exist around any set of societal problems. Taxing policies are notorious for producing unintended distortions. Allegedly it is fairer, for example, to fund schools in a state through a statewide income or sales tax rather than through local property taxes. The main reason given is that there are wide disparities in local property values, and overreliance on the property tax would be unfair to a variety of groups, including farmers and older people. Yet a heavy income tax burden or high sales tax may disproportionately disadvantage poor people because their small incomes are all they have to live on.

•••• Beyond readily detectable shortfalls like the three just mentioned are others such as unforeseen costs that accrue over time in the wake of a new policy, or the way in which a particular policy begins to undercut an equally valid prescription in a related area. For example, few would question the value of implementing special education laws, measures designed to provide needed educational services for disabled citizens. Yet the expanding allocation of resources to serve the needs of disabled students almost inevitably erodes government's capacity - and willingness - to fulfill the educational needs of students without special needs. The biggest losers are those who are unlikely to attend college or to pursue vocational training.

• • • •   As a general rule, almost all policies become outmoded and in need of overhaul in a surprisingly short period of time after they are effected. This is because the collective human response to a new policy often distorts the intended effects of the measure and maybe even other measures it was supposed to complement. To meet legitimate needs amid great constraint, citizens take reasonable actions in response to a new policy. Those actions reverberate back upon the new policy. The effects are much like a game of table pool. The new policy is the cue ball. Citizen actions are the colored balls. When hit, i.e. affected by the new policy, they shoot off in different directions around the table. Sometimes one comes back, hits the cue ball and propels it to a new spot, maybe even sinks it in a pocket. A "scratch" is not a positive outcome. At the very least it signals the need to begin over.

The reaction, for example, of ordinary citizens to the availability of new resources for serving special needs students has made an already tight financial situation into a very taut one in many parts of the country. Many parents, seeing a chance to secure individualized benefits for their children, aggressively sought to have them classified as eligible for special education. Especially parents of learning disabled students, a large group whose claims of eligibility for special services are more tenuous than others, seized this opportunity. As larger numbers of these constituents tapped into already restricted resources, the plight of all students taken together became slightly worse than it was before the well-intentioned moves to aid those with special needs. The result in some parts of the country has been a political backlash against high levels of support for disabled students.

In sum, making policy does have some of the indelible earmarks of one of my father's favorite expressions, "The road to hell is paved with good intentions." A less religious but equally graphic analogy is that of a cat chasing its tail. Round and round the cat runs, seeking to grasp the prize; the faster it goes and harder it tries, the more out of reach the prize becomes. Unintended consequences of deliberate policy moves - or in some cases the absence of consequences from more or less deliberate moves - keep policy makers from the fulfillment of their aims. Higher costs than anticipated, misdirected resources, larger groups of eligible clients than expected, all undermine original intent. So too does the repetitive refrain of constituents, "This policy doesn't apply to me because I'm doing it already anyway." What we may be left with is a sense of despair, that we are in fact not architects of our own fate. Or if we are, we have much learning yet to do before we can craft policy that actually achieves the positive ends we have in mind.

The policy issues Anrig chose to work on were attached to a set of deeply personal concerns that dominated his thoughts and colored his actions throughout his life. The formal language that defined these issues in academic, and even political circles, cloaked for him some very simple values. These values drove him with such great force that he chose to bring his whole being to bear in a most focussed way upon them.

First there was the contention that at the heart of schooling was teaching and learning. For Anrig, this contention was experiential. It grew out of his own experience in Tenafly. It mirrored his response to his teachers in school and others he found outside in foster homes and at camp. His early years had indeed reflected the Taoist expression that when the learner is ready, the teacher will come.

At the same time, this persistent contention offered Anrig a perpetual opportunity to test his mettle as manager and leader. "Teaching and learning" was the ready and right answer to the most appropriate, yet all too infrequently asked question: what is our mission, or more simply, what are we working for? Management guru Peter Drucker asserted that this was the one question an executive should repeatedly ask of himself and the enterprise in his charge (Drucker 1974).

From his work as a camp counselor, school teacher and principal, Anrig knew that teaching and learning was the most integral work of schools. As he headed off from direct contact with young people and teachers to the more diffuse policy arenas of Washington, Boston and Princeton, the challenges of raising and getting an earnest answer to this core question became daunting. After all, bureaucracies, legislative bodies and courts easily slip into self-serving modes and leave behind the essential purposes for which they were created. To the contrary Anrig delighted in asking the question at uncomfortable moments and demanding politely that it be addressed.

Second was civil rights, equality of educational opportunity, particularly for people who had been denied it because of race, native language or gender. For Anrig this issue went hand-in-hand with the centrality of teaching. If teaching and learning were so much a mandate for human beings to function as such, then every person should have access to them in roughly the same amounts.

The principle of equal opportunity is a key that opens the door for all to teaching and learning.   For Anrig, opportunity was what he was granted in Tenafly; and it was especially consequential because he lived under somewhat stressful conditions. Therefore it was what everybody, especially those living under somewhat stressful conditions, should have. It is pretty simple, a matter of fairness, of fair treatment of the less powerful by the more powerful.

When Anrig saw in the formative years of his educational career an opportunity to work on this issue - at Battle Hill School in White Plains, and then in earnest on a much broader front in a Federal agency operating under a new national mandate - he seized it and engaged fully with it. He went at the challenge with even greater determination and resolve in Massachusetts and continued with unabated intensity and persistence at ETS.

He was a persistent warrior on behalf of civil rights throughout his professional career. Although it would be viewed as unusual positioning today, he served as such while an official inside government bureaucracies or large scale establishment organizations. He consciously chose not to play the role of outsider perpetually pleading with government leaders. He chose instead to become a government leader, and to advocate for civil rights from within.

There are few such warriors left, those with the audacity and resolve to think that it is the express role of government and affiliated organizations to fight for the rights of the oppressed as vehemently as community activists do. Sandra Lynch, in recalling her role as General Counsel, noted that Anrig asked her to set up an advocacy office for civil rights within the Massachusetts Department of Education. In the present context, establishing a unit inside government to plead for the individual rights of disabled students and their parents, of Spanish- speaking and African American youth and of girls in male-dominated educational environments, might seem slightly odd.

More than nostalgia prompts me to ask if we as citizens in a democracy have not lost a great deal because of the removal, resignation or retirement - forced or voluntary - of an entire cadre of "insider-advocates" like Anrig. There is not only the loss of the functions they performed from their insider positions. There may be a deeper loss, that of balance and civility in the conduct of public affairs. With a mix of insiders and outsiders bearing the same message, there is less possibility of distressed populations feeling bereft and alienated with no recourse but to stridency and violence. This may be particularly true as we move away from the raw prejudice evidenced in the early stages of civil rights activism into more advanced stages characterized by subtle forms of discrimination.

Do we need such warriors for civil rights in governmental leadership positions today? The *de facto* answer is apparently not, since there are few if any left. But the inclinations, values and actions of our public affairs leaders are a constant source of concern about which we as citizens are agitated, conflicted and confused. It is time to reopen the debate in full force and ask again what kind of people we want to do the people's business and how we want it done.

There is a deeper lesson to be drawn from the unusual role that Anrig chose to play in the fight for civil rights. It is quite simply that he was right in one very important sense, the issue of fair treatment of all citizens will not go away. It might be muted, toned down or suppressed for a while, but it will not go away. Some of our citizens may seek with all their resources and influence to push it aside, to deny it, deflect it, or defer it; but it will not go away. A passing glance at the experience of South Africa over the last several decades ought to provide clear enough instruction that the denial of rights does not result in the dissipation of the energies of the oppressed. Even if they turn underground for short or long periods, they eventually become resurgent.

Anrig saw the third issue - state, federal and local roles in educational decision making - as a critical balance wheel, determining the effectiveness of government operations overall. The knotty questions posed by the issue were what government should be responsible for as opposed to other providers and, more particularly, which level of government should be responsible for what. For Anrig matters such as these fit well with his natural inclination to figure out how to involve several parties in sharing responsibility for leadership. He was rarely concerned about different levels of government having a piece of the action on an issue. He was, in contrast, perpetually preoccupied with organizing and coordinating the efforts of all for the most positive effects (Collected Speeches 1973-81).

Implicit in this issue is the assumption that coherence in managing our public affairs - or at the very least, the establishment of complementary relationships to fulfill common aims - is possible. Also that it is possible to arrive at a proper mix of responsibilities and commitments among governmental levels that will make for a positive and productive use of energies. For a person dedicated to the idea of asking "not what his country could do for him, but what he could do for his country", this was a fertile subject, one which often found its way into his speeches and governed his actions in his last three major jobs.

Anrig did not like to waste energy - his own or anyone else's, particularly when it meant the loss of important benefits to people who did not have much to begin with. He subscribed to the idea that government's essential reason for being was to guarantee opportunity to those, who if they had it, could use it to pull themselves together.

This combination of a need to maximize human energy, a commitment to complementary relationships, and a belief in government's compensatory role led him to a couple of conclusions. One was that each of the three levels of government had a responsibility to lead in areas where the other two could not. Leadership did not just entail picking up the slack for fellow paddlers. Rather it meant getting out in front of swells, cresting them before they produced disabling conditions. This, for example, was why he fought so hard for state aid reform in Massachusetts, knowing all the while that solutions in this area are ephemeral. Whatever the ultimate effects, the effort to fix state aid had existential benefits. It offered needed material assistance at a critical time of high demand for educational services and provided a framework for future work on issues of financial equity.

In addition, shared responsibility worked best when all parties to a task took on a disproportionate share of the burden, rather than sitting back and waiting for others to pitch in. His constant urgings of local leaders to get out ahead on special education before the state and federal governments weighed in with mandates is a good example.

Finally, there is the issue of assessment. In terms that Anrig would have likely found valid, the crux of the issue is the reaches of human accomplishment, the boundaries, dimensions and parameters thereof. Most aptly put by W. Willard Wirtz, U.S. Secretary of Labor in the Johnson Administration, "testing is the hard labor of implementing educational goals." It stands at the crossroads of human aspirations to learn and grow, by offering verification that one has indeed accomplished these.

Anrig had no great passion for testing. In fact his natural bent, as already mentioned, was to be opposed to it. But he did have a great passion for policy. And testing in the early eighties was a very rich ground for the formulation of educational policy. Almost every state, as well as the federal government, was hatching or growing a large testing program, in the belief that the way to influence the schools was to assess them and the students in them. One of Anrig's greatest contributions was to dispel this notion, while at the same time arguing for testing programs that fostered positive educational outcomes. He repeatedly stated that while assessment was integral to moving things forward, it could never substitute for designing and implementing better educational programs (Collected Speeches, 1981-93).

Appropriately, there were a few relatively simple and commonsensical assessment questions Anrig had for the field of assessment itself. Did it advance the craft of teaching and add to students' learning? Was it fair to all who were assessed, both as to what was assessed and the means of administration? Whichever level of government was doing the assessing, did their assessments help them do their job better? To the reader who knows little about education, these questions might appear to be elaborating the obvious. Yet the last ten years of education policy making would lead one to believe that this sort of questioning was not as frequent an occurrence as it should have been.

Selected states, for example, have chosen to test all fourth graders to a level of detail that would best be left to local school leaders. Tests are designed and given not to measure performance per se but to array the test takers along a curve, to separate the wheat from the chaff as it were. The content and language of some test questions violate the cultural norms of certain groups thus making it less likely that respondents in this group will do well on the test.

Because its coverage is broad in terms of the number and diversity of people touched, testing must be done fairly. Its results must be used appropriately by the entity doing the testing. And it must reinforce rather than detract from or be peripheral to the core function of teaching and learning. It must epitomize these qualities for obvious ethical reasons and for less obvious practical ones. Fairly drawn and administered tests make for less wastage of the sum total of available human resources. The desired result is a talent pool that includes the array of capabilities to do the job of living well with each other in the caring embrace of the planet that houses us.

Is there leadership here - focusing on the key roles of teacher and learner, i.e. committing to put forth one's best intellectually and socially; making sure that as many people as possible are allowed to put forth their best; determining periodically whether people and programs are in fact putting out their best as a way of being sure they will continue to do so; and making all levels of government a fit ally in achieving all of the above? Yes, in fact, were these four framed as pithy expressions, they could easily become a code of sound public affairs leadership. It would be applicable whether one were a top line executive or a middle manager, whether one worked in an education organization, a social service agency or health care facility.

Beyond his considerable intellectual and practical contributions on each of these major policy issues lies another important contribution: Anrig's framing of the issues, singly and jointly, in simple terms that all could understand and his earnest attempts at resolving them during the course of his life's work. The burden is ours now, a continuing responsibility to raise up the issues as forthrightly as Anrig did, to engage with them as actively as he did, and to be as clearheaded in proposing solutions as he was. The issues are certainly enduring enough to serve as guideposts for the establishment of an agenda of consequence into the next century.

Chapter 10

CLOSINGS

Summary of Contributions

The working life of Gregory Anrig serves as an indispensable navigational aid for the expeditions of future explorers into the reaches of public affairs leadership. Charting three decades of collective concern about the quality of education, his life offers some useful headings for the work of the next century.

His leadership grew out of direction setting on four key issues: the first line importance of teaching and learning in schools, equality of educational opportunity, the balance among the three levels of government as forces to improve schooling, and the use of assessment to galvanize educational improvement.

From the mid-sixties to the mid-nineties, Anrig worked at defining and disposing with regard to these four major issues. He pondered them and wrote and spoke about them with great clarity and force. But he spent most of his energy acting on them. Predictably the issues molded him as well. As the years unfolded and he became more sophisticated in his views and more influential in the public forum, the principles that guided his work and thinking, did not become more numerous and complex. Rather they winnowed to a few simple propositions. They became his external "anchors to windward", his internal "compass bearings" and ultimately his life's justification and meaning. In more than an incidental way these simple propositions are captured in his "ten commandments of leadership", and in a less formal way in the multiple "Anrigisms" presented at the end of this final chapter.

Anrig clearly sought out the "higher stakes games", where the action was, where people were exercising power to affect the direction of human affairs, where there were resources that could benefit people, where the further development of mankind was on the line. He gravitated to venues where society was at an intriguing crossroad, where there was about to be major controversy, where it was "our turn in the barrel" - one colleague's description of the position of ETS when Anrig took over as President (Brodsky 1994).

He did not seek to be where the action was for the sheer thrill of it or for any potential personal gain related to it. Rather it was where he thought he belonged, because it was where his talents could best be deployed and his principles applied for the greatest benefit. To a large extent he was right. For when he arrived at a "hot spot", he got a lot done, and inspired others to do more than they ever thought they could.

He led, by infusing important institutions with the purpose and meaning for which they had been established. The Federal Office of Education as strong oar in the pull for Civil Rights; the Massachusetts Department of Education as guarantor of equal access, the Educational Testing Service as an aid to teaching and learning - none was clear until he insisted that it became so.

There was always in him an overarching commitment to act for the public good, to carry out the public trust, to be of service to his fellow human beings. He did this while in Washington, D.C., Boston and Princeton, as well as other venues along the way.

The overarching lessons of his life are legion. The most enduring are the ways he enriched our view of what public affairs leadership was all about. His courage, persistent principled choosing, restraint in conflict, and commitment to authenticity and action deserve emulation in multiple quarters. Through his actions, recounted here, and his thoughts, memorialized here and in collected speeches and articles, he also contributed immeasurably to our understanding of major education issues. His contributions make him not only an ingenious leader but a masterful politician and gifted political thinker.

What makes his positioning as a signal leader perhaps even more lofty was his modesty and restraint. In an era in which most if not all of our public leaders compulsively seek front page coverage for their daily deeds and words, he shunned it. Knowing that what he was working on would likely get some media attention, he viewed "back-page coverage" as more desirable. It usually indicated that one was working quietly on the hard issues. In fact, he opined frequently that while his name might appear on page twenty-three, his effect on consequential decisions would likely be front and center. He said it best:

> The headlines come from the issues, not from me. How can I deal with people if they feel I'm trying to get the one-up on them? I don't change my position to fit the group or the situation. I'm not worried about my image. (Pave 1981)

If leadership is, as one writer recently noted, "a willingness to accept responsibility for the future," (Drath and Pallus 1994) then Anrig exhibited it in full measure. He acted well in his time with the future perpetually in mind. Most important for us, the lessons of his life, if incorporated into our present, can make the future a better one than most of us can see in this last half of the last decade of the twentieth century.

Uncovering Meaning in a Life

To summarize Anrig's legacy as a public affairs leader may in fact suffice for the purposes for which this book was written. Nonetheless I feel compelled to go farther, to a point where the reader might join me in peeling away some of the layers of the man's accomplishments and arrive at the core, the essential meaning of his life.

What follows is adapted from a speech I delivered in October, 1994. The occasion was the dedication of the Gregory R. Anrig Building on the grounds of the Educational Testing Service in Princeton, New Jersey. I had worked with Anrig for seven years in the seventies, first at the University of Massachusetts/Boston, then at the Massachusetts Department of Education. We kept in regular contact over the eighties and nineties even though he went one way and I another. More than any other person I encountered, he changed the way I thought about myself as a public person. Because his actions were thoroughly consistent with his words, he made certain tenets of public affairs leadership much more coherent and compelling than they would have been if I had read them in a book. He taught me that leadership above all else involves taking responsibility for the welfare of other human beings. In this speech I attempt to convey why he was so successful as a teacher of public affairs leadership.

Over the past several months, as I have pondered this occasion, two questions remained uppermost in my mind. The first - what difference did Greg Anrig's life make? The second - what was there to love about him? As I began to wrestle with these questions, I came to realize that the two are in many ways one and the same question. They can not be treated as if they were separate. The difference that a person's life makes has everything to do with why we love that person.

Let me show why this contention makes sense. It comes down in fact to the single idea of singularity, of ONENESS. Quite simply, Anrig was ONE with the people he dealt with, including family and friends and professional colleagues, both friends and foes, ONE with several issues of his time, and ONE with the flow of his own life taken in historical context.

This is not to say necessarily that he embodied psychological or spiritual harmony in motion. Quite the contrary he had some jarring edges on the outside and some obvious conflicts and tensions on the inside. It was the way he chose to engage with the people and issues in his path that was the source of his oneness. In a world where so many of us are reserved in our interactions with each other, he jumped in with both feet in almost every interaction of his life. Where we tend to hold back, separate ourselves from each other, and play "wait and see", he pushed himself forward and engaged himself with almost no perceptible reservations.

At root was a oneness with other people, from casual acquaintances to colleagues to friends. As I interviewed people over the last few months several spoke of how this essential aspect manifested itself in his physical presence.

Not only did he fill space in a room in proportion to his dimensions and demeanor, he somehow managed to fill others' space as well. He never did this in an offensive, demanding or threatening way, but rather artfully, benevolently inviting those around him to a place outside themselves where they might be allowed the luxury of less fear.

One of those interviewed was Andrea Ossip, who as a child was a student of Anrig's at Eastview Junior High School in White Plains where he had been a teacher. Interestingly the two had met much earlier. Anrig, it turned out, had taught her to tie her shoes when she was four and he a teenage camp counselor. Using the nickname the kids applied to him at Eastview, Andrea noted:

"Red was my homeroom teacher for three years. In that time I never had him for a class, but he managed to give me a sense that it was OK to be me, he made me feel safe, he treated me with respect, humor and seriousness." (Ossip 1994)

At the heart of this oneness with various people in his life was his humor. His high school newspaper, _The Echo_, captured this angle perfectly when it summarized one of his most significant contributions to school life. "If you hear a quiet classroom suddenly break into laughter, someone there in that room is Greg Anrig" (_The Echo_ 1949).

There is perhaps no more important oneness in life than that which is achievable with one's mate. For Anrig a bond of over thirty years with his wife Charlotte made up this oneness. Together they built a foundation of love and mutual support, and crafted tight bonds in a family that eventually included three children. Two images from their wedding day represent well what *they were able to achieve in the years that followed (Anrig, Charlotte 1994).*

At the time they decided to marry, Charlotte was a kindergarten teacher. Because the wedding was taking place in her home town of Deep River, Connecticut, and because it would make for a pleasant and fitting touch, she invited her entire class to the ceremony. As it turned out, all of them showed up. After the ceremony she asked them to line up - kindergartners know how to do this well - and she went down the line and shook their hands and thanked them for coming.

Years later one of her husband's trademark gestures kept Charlotte's example from their wedding day alive. At the places he worked, he went on extended rounds a few days before Christmas. On these rounds he would shake the hands of every man, woman and child he could find, thank them for their contributions, and wish them a good holiday. This sort of behavior on the part of an executive might not strike anyone as unusual - but for the fact that at a place like the Educational Testing Service there were over a thousand hands to shake.

*The wedding ceremony over, the wedding party left the church. The groom now graciously escorted the bride to a waiting car. He opened the passenger door for her, and she got in. He then proceeded to get in beside her, the **wrong side** since HE was the intended driver. Fully embarrassed - and red-faced to prove it - he quickly jumped out of the car and ran around to the other side. Finally, with each in the proper seat, they drove off together.*

Taken together, this set of moves could be seen as a metaphor for the way their entire relationship unfolded. Greg seeks to join Charlotte on her side. But they both arrive at the understanding that he is to be the more visible doer in the world. He assumes that role with a mix of willingness and reluctance, but with great humor and aplomb. Together they share the journey.

Anrig did not reserve the total engagement of which he was capable for more personal and informal interchanges only. He also exhibited it on occasions that called for consequential self presentation. Job interviews were one such occasion. A particularly exemplary one of these occurred when he was a candidate for the presidency of Educational Testing Service, a post he was successful in securing.

Some said, partially tongue in cheek, that he won the job because of a casual postscript that appeared in a letter of reference Francis Keppel had written to the ETS Board on his behalf. Keppel was U.S. Commissioner of Education under President Kennedy and Harvard Dean of Education under James Conant. "You may be surprised," wrote Keppel, "by the first appearance. His beaming face and rotund figure make one think of one's favorite bartender. He is in fact a sober and serious man" (Keppel 1980).

The real reason I believe Anrig was chosen for the ETS job, from among 600 applicants, including 60 present and former college presidents and 6 Rhodes Scholars, was what John Hennessey said about him. Hennessey is a distinguished professor at Dartmouth's Tuck School of Business and former head of the ETS Board. He led the "search committee" that was charged with finding a successor to William Turnbull as ETS President in 1981. "He wasn't in a job interview. He got caught up in being one of us. In being a real resource to us he swept us up. He told us what he had done that would fit with the job and what he had done that would not. He evidenced remarkable instincts about what the ETS presidency would demand, thereby rearranging our own view of the selection criteria. He willingly exposed himself to our gaze. He was a whole person, perfectly pleased to be part of the process. He was so valid" (Hennessey 1994).

For those of you who have been in challenging interview situations, I think you would agree that these are conditions worth creating if one were interested in impressing one's interviewers. Ironically, to create them so profoundly requires a subjugation of the ego, a genuine willingness to meet the needs of others and an ability to detach from one's own personal concerns about attaining a positive outcome. This is the essence of Hennessey's commentary.

Anrig was as much one with the great social issues he joined as he was with the people he encountered. His life manifested a striking oneness with several of the abiding issues *of American education, issues of substance and duration, grand enough both to pre-date and to outlive him.*

Charlotte Anrig was kind enough to give me all of his professional papers - for he himself was thinking about writing a book at the time he became ill and died. The choices he made about what to set aside in those half dozen boxes were illuminating. One that caught my eye was the text of a speech, the only self-standing set of remarks in all of the papers. It was delivered by the then U.S. Commissioner of Education, Harold "Doc" Howe in 1967 in Cincinnati. Howe was Anrig's boss at the time and, perhaps more important, his mentor on the matter of exemplary work in the field of civil rights.

In the talk Howe issued a call to arms for state and local leaders to take up the charge against segregation in the schools. He called the tide of new federal education laws just passed new leverage against old ingrained problems, segregation not the least among them. At the end of the speech Howe called for a drive for equal educational opportunity that had entered a critical phase. "Today it is at last being waged in the only places and the only way that can determine the ultimate outcome, in the states and local communities and at state and local initiative" (Howe 1967).

Right next to that speech in Anrig's papers was a report of the Stanford Research Institute, dated 1977, ten years after Howe's speech. In essence, the report said, "except for the handful of leaders already identified, states seem unlikely to voluntarily pursue desegregation on their own. Desegregation issues are politically sensitive and few political leaders appear willing to press them" (The State Role in School Desegregation 1977).

One of the states mentioned in the report as willing to press the issue of desegregation was Massachusetts. There, the State Board of Education had waged a ten-year battle with Boston School officials, from 1965 to 1974, to secure their compliance with racial balance standards. Then, in 1974, Federal Judge Arthur Garrity assumed responsibility for effecting a fit remedy in the Boston desegregation case.

Anrig was the head education official in Massachusetts from the early 70's to the early 80's. During that time, fully one with the issue at hand, he threw himself headlong into the fray that unfolded around school integration in that racially divided city. He pulled every lever his position afforded. And he urged the State Board, and through them the Federal Court, to do all they could to guarantee the rights of Black children to "due process of law", i.e. adequate schooling.

After seven long years of intense work to desegregate the Boston Schools, outgoing State Education Commissioner Anrig wrote Judge Garrity in 1981. The topic was how the Federal Court might finally disengage from the internal affairs of the Boston Public Schools. Garrity, as he had with other communications from Anrig, found the letter compelling and implemented most of the recommendations in it in the years that followed (Garrity 1994).

When I interviewed him in the fall of 1994, Judge Garrity talked at length about the Boston case. At the end of the interview, he presented me with a souvenir, a copy of one of the orders issued in the case. With a slight twinkle in his eye, he noted, "you probably think the case is closed after all this time, it's not; this is what I hope will be the next to last order" (Garrity 1994).

The previous few paragraphs are at best cursory snapshots of twenty seven years of dogged persistence, of tenacity in pursuit, from 1967 to 1994. What is telling about them is that they reveal a oneness, a full fledged engagement of a person with an issue of magnitude, complexity and consequence, an issue of social justice. Anrig sought and accomplished this oneness much as he had with family, friends, colleagues and employers.

Finally, I argue that Anrig achieved a oneness with history. In one of his speeches there is an excerpt from a speech Horace Mann had delivered in 1859, a few weeks before his death. Anrig chose to use Mann's words to conclude an address he was making a hundred and twenty years later to Massachusetts School Committee Members and School Superintendents. The context for Anrig's talk was the looming shadow of Proposition 2 1/2, a measure to effect a property tax cap in every locality much like Proposition 13 in California. Mann had said:

"I pant. I yearn for another warfare in behalf of right, in hostility to wrong where without furlough and without going into winter quarters I would enlist for another fifty years' campaign and fight it out for the glory of God and the welfare of man. To a certain extent you are to live for yourselves in this life. To a greater extent you are to live for others. And I beseech you to treasure up in your hearts these my parting words. Be ashamed to die until you have won some victory for humanity" (Anrig 1979).

Horace Mann was the acknowledged father of public education in America and he was the first Commissioner of Education for the Commonwealth of Massachusetts. When Anrig left that post in 1981 several commentators openly compared him to Mann. Anrig died in 1993 after three decades of service to American education. Mann's parting words appropriately capture the commitments of one of his most promising successors.

"Anrigisms"

Greg Anrig would not have dubbed himself a philosopher, yet he clearly had a philosophy. Being more addicted to action than deliberation, his philosophy was revealed *in media res*, i.e. in the middle of things, in the form of sayings he held dear. One of the people I interviewed for the book eschewed these sayings suggesting that they represented "leadership by tritism." I do not concur. On the contrary I find some grains of truth and even wisdom in them. So here is the most complete list of "Anrigisms" I was able to compile, from both my memory and that of others:

• • • •   As a former history major in college, or as a junior high school trombone player - no Board meeting went by without these introductory references, mildly self-deprecatory invocations of the knowledge and experience he brought with him to tackle tough issues; his "credentials" as it were.

• • • •   Brown Helmet Session - a term of suspiciously profane origin, denoting a discussion with a colleague - boss as well as subordinate - about what he or she should not have done and probably ought not to consider doing again.

•••• Checks and balances - the most ingenious architecture of the U.S. Constitution in his view; these provided fertile ground for the creative tensions that helped institutions and levels of government work for the common good.

•••• Cheers! Cheers! Cheers! - the verbal equivalent of several slaps on the back, words used to close a handwritten note of congratulations for accomplishment or attainment; more than a slight connotation of large glasses filled with spirited liquid.

•••• Closure - what every business discussion should have at the end, including next steps.

•••• Controversy and public scrutiny - that which he had become used to when he arrived at ETS, i.e. Harry Truman's "kitchen".

•••• Credibility, if you haven't built it over time, you'll never have it when you need it - a reflection on the powerfully negative response of a legislative body or a press corps to a proposal by a public official at a moment when the official's whole program is on the line and he needs support.

•••• Creative tensions - see "checks and balances" above.

•••• Dogged perseverance - usually evidenced by paramecia-like creatures operating in the encumbrance-filled world of public affairs.

•••• Education - the running of which is much too important to be left to professional educators.

•••• First-rate - probably the highest praise he could offer for a job well done.

•••• Hot Stove Approach - what some might call "management by walking around" - always done with great vigor, plentiful handshakes, some pecks on the cheek especially for older women, perpetual beads of perspiration on his own forehead.

•••• I lose 90% of my battles, but the other 10% make it worth it - the normal odds on getting things done in the public sector; nonetheless a self-conscious understatement reflecting appropriate modesty and restraint.

•••• I don't have ulcers; the people who work with me do - a self-lampooning way of acknowledging his intensity about task completion combined with his commitment to sharing all the challenges of the job with his associates.

•••• If you make a decision when I'm away, it's mine - a parting comment to those left in charge as he strode out the door for vacation; meant to instill in advance full confidence, deep appreciation, and maybe a slight wisp of apprehension.

•••• Let's take 30 seconds and savor how well we did - a form of "extrinsic" reward shared between him and staff for an extraordinarily difficult job well done.

•••• Like a dog with a dishrag - the way in which one should implement the squinty-eyed view, with great attachment, determination and perseverance.

•••• Oh, is that right? - according to his driver at ETS, this was his favorite expression. It seemed to serve him well as a placeholder in one-on-one conversations. It gave him time to think about the idea being advanced so that he could frame a fit response.

•••• One person's mandate is another person's right - his response to the groundswell in the early 80's directed at State Governments across the nation, "no mandates without money."

•••• Overwhelming - one of a few great "no-no's" that a person could use to characterize the challenges of a job; the equivalent of "hand wringing", virtually no problem deserved this modifier.

•••• My hero is the paramecium - with the simplest sense of purpose the paramecium keeps going until it finds an opening and squeezes through; the ultimate analogy for what it takes to administer well on behalf of the public.

•••• Politics - not a dirty word; Webster called it "the art of governing".

•••• Prepare for a board meeting the same way you prepare for testimony before a U.S. Congressional Committee - complete dedication to doing well by one's board of trustees because the quality of its deliberations relates directly to the quality of staff presentations.

•••• Round robin's barn - derision for the perambulatory arguments of a person who either does not want to or can not get to the point in a discussion of some import.

•••• Speeches rarely change anybody's thinking - born of an awareness that speeches are inherently ineffective as teaching devices, and that they better assist the speech maker to clarify his own thoughts rather than the listeners'.

•••• Squinty-eyed view - clear focus on the few things a public affairs leader should and can get done rather than the multiple things that ought to be done but can not be accomplished all at once.

•••• Take the rest of the night off - normally offered to a working colleague after 9 P.M. to cap off a day fraught with crisis, frustration and temporary setback.

•••• That's two ... - strikes, that is. This was usually delivered to sound like "Here's Johnny" (Carson) and meant as a warning regarding major bloopers not to be repeated.

•••• When besieged or in doubt, ATTACK! - a frequent suggestion, only partially "tongue in cheek", for handling a difficult set of circumstances surrounding a complex social issue.

•••• Wrong to refuse to fire a person because of his race as to refuse to hire a person because of his race - a reminder to himself as he was deliberating a particularly difficult personnel decision.

•••• You done good! - what his former English teacher said in response to top-notch performance.

Bibliography

Albright, R., former Educational Testing Service Senior Vice President and former head of an historically Black university, interview by author, May 2, 1994, Princeton, NJ, notes in the hands of the author.

Anonymous, multiple interviews by author, 1994, notes in the hands of the author.

Anrig, C. (Chris), Anrig's youngest son, interview by author, October 13, 1994, Princeton, NJ, notes in the hands of the author.

Anrig, C. (Charlotte), Anrig's wife, interviews by author, multiple dates over 1994-5, Princeton, NJ, New York, NY and Needham, MA, notes in the hands of the author.

Anrig, G., Collected Speeches, May 2, 1973 to June 18, 1993, two binders in the hands of the author, quoted excerpts from the following:

_____. A speech entitled "A Tiger Returns", First Distinguished Alumni Award Dinner, Tenafly High School, Tenafly, NJ, May 7, 1987.

_____. A speech entitled "What Parents Ought to Know About Standardized Testing and College Admission in American Education", National Parent Teachers Association Annual Conference, Washington, D.C., June 18, 1985.

_____. A speech entitled "Local Control and State Responsibility: Keeping the Tensions Creative", IDEA Fellows Program, Agnes Scott College, Decatur, GA, Stephens College, Columbia, MO, Harvey Mudd College, Claremont, CA and The Kamehameha Schools, Honolulu, HA, June 13-19, 1980.

_____. A speech entitled "Leadership for the Eighties", National Community Education Conference, Washington, D.C., November 29, 1979.

_____. A speech entitled "What's Right With Public Education", Massachusetts Association of School Committees and Massachusetts Association of School Superintendents Joint Conference, Hyannis, MA, October 24, 1979.

_____. A speech entitled "Boston and the South - Differences and Similarities in School Desegregation", Boston, MA, exact date unknown - late 1974, early 1975.

_____. A speech entitled "Education in Boston: Past, Present and Future", Boston Rotary Club Meeting, Boston, MA, September 5, 1973.

_____. A speech entitled "Directions for Education in 1974 - State and Local Leadership", Massachusetts Association of School Committees and Massachusetts Association of School Superintendents Joint Conference, Hyannis, MA, October 17, 1973.

_____. A speech entitled "Conversations from Wingspread", The Johnson Foundation, Racine, WI, n.d.

Anrig, G., Boston, MA to the Honorable W. Arthur Garrity, Jr., Boston, MA, July 6, 1981, copy in the hands of the author.

Anrig, G., Needham, MA to Theodore M. Black, Chancellor, New York State Board of Regents, Roselyn, NY, May 23, 1977, copy in the hands of the author.

Anrig, G., Needham, MA to Chester Finn, Washington, D.C., March 26, 1977, copy in the hands of the author.

Anrig, G., Needham, MA to Stephen Kaagan, New York, NY, March 4, 1978, original in the hands of the author.

Anrig, G., Boston, MA to Joe Nyquist, Albany, NY, December 7, 1976, copy in the hands of the author.

Anrig, G., Boston, MA, confidential memorandum to Massachusetts State Board of Education, Boston, MA, March 25, 1974, copy in the hands of the author.

APA Monitor, Vol. 18, No. 1, January, 1987.

Bell, T.H., former U.S. Secretary and Commissioner of Education under Presidents Reagan and Ford respectively, phone interview by author, October 13, 1994, Salt Lake City, UT, notes in the hands of the author.

Brodsky, D., former Educational Testing Service Senior Vice President, interviews by author, May 5, 1994 and October 12, 1994, Princeton, NJ, notes in the hands of the author.

Bowker, J., Educational Testing Service Vice President, interview by author, October 14, 1994, Princeton, NJ, notes in the hands of the author.

Campbell, A., former Educational Testing Service Board Member and ARA executive, interview by author, March 11, 1994, Philadelphia, PA, notes in the hands of the author.

Carlton, S., Educational Testing Service test developer, interview by author, Princeton, NJ, October 12, 1994, notes in the hands of the author.

Chauncey, H., first President of the Educational Testing Service, interview by author, September 3, 1994, Shelburne, VT, notes in the hands of the author.

Cole, N., President of the Educational Testing Service, 1993-, interview by author, May 3, 1994, Princeton, NJ, notes in the hands of the author.

Cohen, M, former Boston Globe education reporter, interview by author, September 1, 1994, Brookline, MA, notes in the hands of the author.

Daly, M., former Massachusetts Deputy Commissioner of Education, interviews by author, June 20, 1994 and December 1, 1994, Boston, MA, notes in the hands of the author.

Darling-Hammond, L, Professor, Columbia University Teachers College, phone interview by author, August 15, 1994, New York, NY, notes in the hands of the author.

Deng Ming-Dao, <u>Tao, Daily Meditations</u>, Harper Collins, San Francisco, CA, 1992.

Drath, W. and Pallus, C., <u>Making Common Sense, Leadership as Meaning-making in a Community Of Practice</u>, Center for Creative Leadership, Greensboro, NC, 1994.

Drucker, P., <u>Management: Tasks, Practices, Responsibilities</u>, Random House, New York, NY, 1974.

<u>The Echo</u>, Tenafly New Jersey High School Newspaper, 1949.

Elmore, R. and McLaughlin, M., <u>Steady Work: Policy, Practice, and the Reform of American Education</u>, National Institute of Education Series #R-3574-NIE/RC, Rand Corporation, Santa Monica, CA, 1988.

Francis, N., former Educational Testing Service Board Member and President of Xavier University in New Orleans, interview by author, March 27, 1995, New Orleans, LA, notes in the hands of the author.

Fuhrman, S., Designing Coherent Educational Policy: Improving the System, Jossey-Bass, San Francisco, CA, 1993.

Garrity, A., Federal District Judge, semi-retired, interview by author, September 1, 1994, Boston, MA, notes in the hands of the author.

Grier, A., Educational Testing Service administrator, interview by author, October 12, 1994, Princeton, NJ, notes in the hands of the author.

Grigsby, C., former chairman of the Massachusetts State Board of Education, interview by author, December 1, 1994, Boston, MA, notes in the hands of the author.

Hanford, G., former President of The College Board, interview by author, October 27, 1994, Washington, D.C., notes in the hands of the author.

Hennessey, J., former Educational Testing Service Board Member and Distinguished Professor, The Amos Tuck School of Business Administration, Dartmouth University, interview by author, September 2, 1994, Hanover, NH, notes in the hands of the author.

Hennessey, J., Hanover, NH to Gregory Anrig, March 26, 1981, Boston, MA, original in the hands of the author.

Hennessey, J., "External Views of ETS", A Confidential Report to the Board of Trustees of the Educational Testing Service, Princeton, NJ, December 1, 1986, copy in the hands of the author.

Hennessey, J., "Summary of Report to the Board of Trustees, Educational Testing Service, on Behalf of the Presidential Search Committee (Confidential), Atlanta, GA, March 17, 1981, copy in the hands of the author.

Horne, E., Secretary to the Educational Testing Service Board of Trustees, multiple interviews by author, 1994-5, Princeton, NJ, notes in the hands of the author.

Howe, H., Educational Testing Service Board Member and former U.S. Commissioner of Education under President Johnson, phone interview by author, March 20, 1994, Harvard, MA, notes in the hands of the author.

Howe, H., speech entitled "A New Focus For School Desegregation", Forum of the Jewish Community Center, Cincinnati, OH, December 6, 1967, copy in the hands of the author.

Issues and Observations, Center for Creative Leadership, Vol.14, No.3, Greensboro, NC, 1994.

Jackson, E., advocate for the rights of Black children during the Boston desegregation crisis, presently an administrator at Northeastern University, Boston, MA, interview by author, December 1, 1994, Boston, MA, notes in the hands of the author.

Kaagan, S., Stovall, B., Hesterman, O. and Catala, Y. "Bonding Two Cultures, University and Community, through Leadership Development in The Journal of Leadership Studies, Vol.2, No.3, Summer, 1995.

Keppel, F., Cambridge, MA to John Hennessey, Hanover, NH, December 17, 1980, copy in the hands of the author.

Knott, K. and Freeman, F. "Leadership Education in Colleges and Universities" in Issues and Observations, Vol 14, No. 3, Center for Creative Leadership, 1994.

Kofman, F. and Senge, P. "Communities of Commitment: The heart of learning organizations" in Organizational Dynamics, Vol 22, No. 3, 1993.

LaPointe, A., National Assessment of Education Progress Director at ETS, interview by author, October 14, 1994, Princeton, NJ, notes in the hands of the author.

Leadership, Anrig's Ten Commandments, Pamphlet of the Institute for Educational Leadership, Washington, D.C., 1994.

Lee,. C. "Followership: The essence of leadership" in Training, January, 1991.

Lynch, S., Circuit Judge, United States Court of Appeals For the First Circuit and former General Counsel in the Massachusetts Department of Education in the 70's, interviews by author, June 20, 1994 and August 31, 1994, Boston, MA, notes in the hands of the author.

Manning, Willie, Anrig's driver at the Educational Testing Service, interview by author, October 13, 1994, Princeton, NJ, notes in the hands of the author.

Manning, Win, former Educational Testing Service Senior Vice President, phone interviews by author, February 7 and 16, 1995, Princeton, NJ, notes in the hands of the author.

McKettrick, F., former colleague and long-time administrator at the U.S. Office and then Department of Education in Washington, D.C., interview by author, July 7, 1994, Washington, D.C., notes in the hands of the author.

Messick, S, Educational Testing Service Distinguished Research Scientist, interview by author, May 3, 1994, Princeton, NJ, notes in the hands of the author.

Moore, T., Care of the Soul, Harper Perennial, NY, 1992.

Narrin, A. and Associates, ETS: The corporation that makes up minds, Ralph Nader, Washington, D.C., 1980.

Nirenberg, John, The Living Organization: Transforming Teams into Workplace Communities, Business One Irwin, Homewood, IL, 1993.

Orfield, G., Harvard University Professor and noted expert on school integration, interview by author, December 1, 1994, Cambridge, MA, notes in the hands of the author.

Ossip, A., former middle school student of Anrig's, phone interview by author, Tarrytown, NY, September 1, 1994, notes in the hands of the author.

O'Toole, J., Leading Change: The Argument for Values-Based Leadership, Jossey-Bass, San Francisco, CA, 1995.

Pave, Marvin. "Education and Hard Work -- it's the basic Anrig mix" Boston Globe Centerpiece, April 7, 1981.

The Phil Donahue Show, November 30, 1981, videotape, 52 minutes, copy in the hands of the author.

Phillips, T., former CEO of New England Life Insurance Co and former Board Member of the Educational Testing Service and the Massachusetts State Board of Education, phone interview by author, March 6, 1995, Weston, MA, notes in the hands of the author.

Pressman, R., an attorney who represented the Black Plaintiffs in the Boston desegregation case, interview by author,

December 2, 1994, Boston, MA, notes in the hands of the author.

Ramsey, P., Educational Testing Service Vice President, interview by author, May 3, 1994, Princeton, NJ, notes in the hands of the author.

Readings from the Hurricane Island Outward Bound School, Rockland, ME, n.d.

Robinson, J., Brookline, MA to Gregory R. Anrig, Boston, MA, February 8, 1980, original in the hands of the author.

Schneider, R., General Counsel at the Massachusetts Department of Education, formerly assistant general counsel in the Department, interview by author, June 20, 1994, Everett, MA, notes in the hands of the author.

Schneider, R. to Gregory R. Anrig, Brookline, MA, August 6, 1981, original in the hands of the author.

Shanker, A., President of the American Federation of Teachers, phone interview by author, January 4, 1995, Washington, D.C., notes in the hands of the author.

Solomon, R., former Educational Testing Service Senior Vice President in the 70's and 80's, interview by author, October 13, 1994, Princeton, NJ, notes in the hands of the author.

Stewart, D., President of The College Board, interview by author, May 4, 1994, New York, NY, notes in the hands of the author.

Terry, R., Authentic Leadership: Courage in Action, Jossey-Bass, San Francisco, CA, 1993.

The State Role in School Desegregation, A report prepared by the Stanford Research Institute for the Office of the Assistant

Secretary for Education, Department of HEW (Research Note 23, EPRC 4537-23), Washington, D.C., July, 1977.

United States District Court, District of Massachusetts, <u>Morgan et al., v. Burke et al.</u>, Civil Action No. 72-911-G, Final Judgment As Amended, Boston, MA, July 19, 1994.

von Mayrhauser, S., Educational Testing Service General Counsel, interview by author, May 2, 1994, Princeton, NJ, notes in the hands of the author.

Weinman, J., former Massachusetts Department of Education colleague and presently Senior Vice-President of The College Board, multiple interviews by author, New York, NY, 1994, notes in the hands of the author.

Willingham, W., Educational Testing Service Distinguished Research Scientist, interview by author, May 2, 1994, Princeton, NJ, notes in the hands of the author.

Wilson, R., staff member of the American Council on Education, interview by author, October 27, 1994, Washington, D.C., notes in the hands of the author.

Wirtz, Willard to John Hennessey, 1980, copy in the hands of the author.

Zeigler, M., Massachusetts special education advocate, interview by author, September 2, 1994, Boston, MA, notes in the hands of the author.

Zurlini, J., high school friend of Anrig, phone interview by author, Tenafly, NJ, October 17, 1994, notes in the hands of the author.

Index

Author's Biographical Sketch

Stephen S. Kaagan since 1991 has been a professor in the College of Education at Michigan State University. He also served as Vice President of the Michigan Partnership for New Education from 1991-1993. Previously, he was a chief state education officer (Vermont Education Commissioner, 1982-1988), academic head of an institution of higher education (Provost, Pratt Institute, 1977-1982), and chief executive of a non-profit educational organization (President, Hurricane Island Outward Bound, 1989-1991). He has been a classroom teacher (Arlington, Massachusetts and Canberra, Australia) and has taught management and organization development courses at Pratt Institute, Rutgers University, and the University of Southern Maine.

Dr. Kaagan has a doctorate from Harvard and a bachelor's from Williams College, as well as two honorary doctorates (Williams College and Green Mountain College).

He has consulted on leadership development, strategic planning, management and organizational development with a number of government and non-profit organizations, and has written extensively on leadership, accountability of schools, and the role of the arts in schooling.